ACING IT!

A Mindful Guide to Maximum Results
on Your College Admissions Test

ERIKA OPPENHEIMER

SAT is a registered trademark of the College Board and The ACT is a registered trademark of ACT, Inc. Neither the College Board nor ACT, Inc. has endorsed this publication.

Some names and identifying details have been changed to respect the privacy of the students referenced in this book.

ISBN: 1514739690
ISBN-13: 978-1514739693

To my teachers,
in the classroom and out.

CONTENTS

A NOTE ON THE NEW SAT AND DIGITAL ACT

The College Board recently announced that it will completely overhaul the SAT. The new test, debuting in spring 2016, will represent a reconfiguring of the SAT. Back to the 1600-point scale. Away with vocab. Limited calculator use in the Math section. Guessing penalty, be gone! In with "real world" math and evidence-based reading and writing.

Meanwhile, the ACT began transitioning from traditional #2 pencils and bubble sheets (so *analog*) to an entirely computer-based test administration in spring 2015.

How do these changes affect the relevance of this book?

Acing It! addresses concepts that span far beyond the nitty-gritty of either test's content or structure, so this book will remain relevant as the tests evolve. Sure, some of the things I cover here—such as differences in format, how to work with the guessing penalty, and why to check your bubble sheet—are subject to change. But I also discuss the physical, emotional, and psychological fundamentals of being a good test taker. The ideas in this book will elevate your testing game because the basics of peak performance don't vary as much as their applications do.

I wrote *Acing It!* in relation to the tests in their current formats, and the next edition will reflect changes to the test formats. Just like the tests themselves, all we can do is take this process one step at a time, doing the best we can with what we know.

CHAPTER 1
LET'S BEGIN

First off: Hello! I'm so excited to be a part of your test prep adventure!

Congratulations on taking this positive step toward success on your college admissions test. I know you have what it takes.

In this chapter, we're going to lay the groundwork for your test prep. I will introduce my test prep approach, discuss the objective purpose of the tests, help you tune in to your personal purpose, and more.

Everything in this chapter will help you to build clarity around the tests, and clarity is key in any creative pursuit. And, lest there be any confusion, test prep *is* a creative pursuit.

Just like an artist who wants to create a painting, you have an idea for something that you want to bring into existence: in this case, positive results on your SAT or ACT, and everything that those results may facilitate. The clearer your vision at the beginning, the more smoothly the rest of the process will go and the better your ability to deal with obstacles as they arise.

This Is Not Your Standard(ized) Prep Book

Imagine going to the test prep section of your local bookstore. What do you see? I'm guessing you envision shelves and shelves of big, fat prep books containing study guides, practice tests, and lots of useful tricks to ensure that you attain a perfect score (okay, maybe 98th percentile) on the test, gain admission to your dream school, and go on to make a positive contribution to the world in a job you love. There might be some flash card decks, too. (Vocab!)

So, what's the deal with this slender "prep" book with nary a practice test to be found? How on Earth will it help you ace the test and lead the life of your dreams?

This prep book is not about the *content* of the SAT, ACT, or any other standardized test. As you very well know, there are lots of those books out there, and the world probably doesn't need another. (Then again, maybe it does. It always bugs me when I find wrong answers in those other books. Five editions and millions of dollars in sales later, wouldn't you think they could fix the typos?)

Nope, this book is about the *context* of the SAT, ACT, and many other tests you will take in your academic career. Heck, it might even help you with some life tests.

What do I mean by "context"? The context is everything happening around the test, including, but not limited to, your attitudes, ideas, habits, environment, friends, family, teachers, dream colleges…even your music collection. Most other books devote about three pages to the context of your test preparation, but the context is the real game-changer in your performance. By establishing a context of good habits—work habits, thinking habits, and physical habits—you can set yourself up for success on tests, including the SAT and ACT.

This book is meant to be a catalyst, a fire-starter—a tool that will help you use all those other books and practice tests more effectively. This book will *prepare* you to prepare.

Even if you've already begun your test prep, I'd recommend reading this book in its entirety, to start. As you read, dog-ear its pages and highlight the ideas that resonate with you so that you can revisit specific sections as they apply to your test prep.

Who Am I?

Since we'll be spending a fair amount of time together, it seems polite that I tell you a little about myself, where I came from, and how I got here.

High School Me

I grew up in Sioux Falls, South Dakota. More of a big-city girl at heart, I always dreamed of leaving the Midwest. Belle and Ariel were my favorite Disney princesses, and, now that I think about it, they shared a curiosity for learning and a desire for something more. A peaceful life in a provincial town—under the sea or above—was not enough for them, or for me.

College seemed to be my ticket out of my hometown. I was determined, a girl on a mission. One night, after my freshman year of high school, I sat awake reading a book by a college admissions consultant. I felt completely overwhelmed. There were other kids out there doing what?!? How would I ever measure up? I was too far behind. Surely doomed. In a panic, I woke my mom around midnight. She assured me that I would be okay and that it would all work out in the end. She went back to bed; I kept reading.

In high school, I was your standard overachiever who felt chronically overlooked no matter how much she achieved. I was in the marching band, concert band, choir (section leader), and highest-ranked a cappella group. I earned the second-highest score among the altos who auditioned for All-State Choir. I competed with our speech team (co-captain). I was on a competitive dance team. I was a charter member of a theater company that performed plays with socially conscious messages at schools. I earned As in all my classes (well, all except for AP U.S. History). I won a national award for writing. For two years, I didn't have a lunch period so I could participate in elective activities or take an extra class.

What didn't I do? I wasn't a student council member, cheerleader, prom queen, debater, or jock. I played soccer in middle school, and, although I often played defense, I was embarrassed by the fact that I had never scored a goal in a game. I never performed in the top concert band. I never made it to Nationals in speech or won the lead in the high school play. The coach of my dance team asked me not to perform at a competition because I couldn't consistently nail a quadruple pirouette. And, even though I was in the advanced classes and had a nearly perfect GPA, even though I grew up to coach students in standardized tests, I did not rank as a National Merit Semifinalist. A part of me viewed these non-accomplishments as failures. Perfectionist much?

I put a lot of pressure on myself to succeed. I strove to do "my best"—or better than my best, as if such a thing existed—whenever possible, and I was determined to use my capacity for hard work to ensure my acceptance at a highly selective college. I had no concept that I was overachieving. I worked hard and felt discouraged when the desired results didn't come or didn't come soon enough. My perspective was often "I am not good enough."

At this point in my life, I was in survival-via-success mode. My focus was on the external markers of achievement: good grades, awards, friends, solos, leading roles. The fact that I was regularly tired, stressed, moody, anxious, and lonely didn't feel good, but those feelings also didn't feel like choices or the results of choices. It didn't occur to me that my habits could influence how calm, open, confident, and joyful I felt. Grades, on the other hand, I could control. So, I kept pushing myself, making it through one challenge, then another, then another, sure that I would feel better after this audition or that test, so long as the result went my way.

On the day I graduated high school, I spent a good 30 percent of my graduation ceremony worried that I had chosen the wrong shoes for the occasion.

College Me

I attended Georgetown University in Washington, DC. I had several amazing professors who inspired me and opened my eyes to a new way of looking at the world. Dr. Steven Sabat was one such professor.

Dr. Sabat taught Physiological Psychology. I didn't choose the class because physiology or anatomy particularly interested me, but because Sabat was regarded as one of the best teachers in the department, and I was a student who actively sought out the best teachers (an approach to class selection I highly recommend).

Sabat demonstrated great respect for his students. He was a firm believer in no surprises. Given that he knew what he wanted us to learn, he figured he might as well tell us before the test, rather than keep it a secret and, later, feel frustrated when we didn't know what he wanted us to know. Before each test, he distributed long lists of questions related to the chapters we had studied, with the promise that some would show up on the exam in the form of short answer and essay questions. Despite knowing the questions ahead of time, the breadth and complexity of the material required me to study more intensely than I ever had before. By the time I finished answering all of the questions, I felt like he might as well have said, "Go study all of the chapters and the lecture notes," but at least I knew more or less what was coming.

When we received our second exam back, my heart sank. I'd received a C. To my overachiever self, it felt horrible. I had never earned a test grade that low in my entire life. I felt defeated. I felt confused. I felt disappointed. I felt generally awful.

I attended Dr. Sabat's office hours determined to figure out how this had happened. I didn't understand: I had stayed up hours and hours preparing for this exam, and it hadn't been enough. Of our four exams, three would count toward our final grades. Sure, Dr. Sabat dropped our lowest test grade, but the C left me with zero room for error moving forward, if I hoped to earn an A for the semester. And, at this point, I didn't trust myself to score well down the line.

Dr. Sabat and I started reviewing the questions I had answered incorrectly. Growing increasingly frustrated as we moved through the test, I began to cry. Dr. Sabat remained calm and compassionate. He listened to me as I lamented that I felt like nothing I did was enough. Once I'd begun to calm down, we started working through the multiple-choice questions. I noticed a few instances in which I had changed my selection from the right answer to a wrong answer. I expressed my frustration: "I thought that was right, but then I changed it."

I will never forget Dr. Sabat's reply: "Next time you think you have the right answer, pretend an angel is telling it to you." Boom. Seriously. Paradigm shift. I'd often been told to "go with my gut," but sometimes my gut felt confused. The idea that it wasn't all up to me and that I was supported made me feel more trusting in the pull toward an answer choice. Sabat's "test angel" was the right advice at the right time. His words not only comforted me, they also gave me hope that the next test could go better. After all, I had an angel on my side.

Post-Grad Me

I began tutoring students in their preparation for college admissions tests while I pursued an acting career in New York City. Initially, I expected the pattern to be teach content, teach skills, get results.

Sure enough, test content and skills were important components of test prep. But I also observed that my students struggled with anxiety, stress, demanding schedules, and attention issues that hindered their progress. The training I'd received as a tutor did not include any practical strategies that would help students deal with these issues; however, I had discovered techniques to cope with these issues in my own life. I began talking students through their challenges and introducing them to various mindfulness practices. The results of this expanded coaching were pretty extraordinary.

For example, there was Jamie, a senior at a top high school in New York City. When she was singing, she felt unstoppable. She was also funny, charismatic, and kind. But when it came to studying—math, in particular—all her insecurities flared up. Jamie had learning differences, including ADHD, which went undiagnosed until she was fifteen. For the majority of her academic career, she sat in math class feeling stupid. Over that time, she built up a lot of negative self-talk.

Jamie wanted to study vocal performance at a top liberal arts university, but to do that she needed to raise her test scores. Before she started working with me, she'd spent several months working with another tutor, and her score barely budged. Add this to her years of feeling inferior in the classroom, and she wasn't all that optimistic about pulling off her college admissions test. In fact, she felt like she was watching her chance to be admitted to her dream school slip through her fingers.

In September of her senior year, I was enlisted to turn Jamie's prep around. We applied the mindfulness techniques and unique learning strategies that I had begun to incorporate into my test preparation program. Not only did her test scores improve, but she felt more capable in school, her Bs turned into As, her confidence shot through the roof, and she began to enjoy learning. The first time Jamie admitted to having fun during a math section, she blushed. Remember, she had spent what felt like her whole life believing that math was hard, she was stupid, and any attempt to experience the subject as anything but arduous would be futile.

When I attended Jamie's senior recital in the spring, her face lit up as she told me that she would be attending her dream college. Once worried that she couldn't learn, even with the help of a tutor, she now had the confidence to move across the country and turn her dreams into reality.

Incorporating the psychology of test prep into the process made it more enjoyable and effective. I helped students to do better and, moreover, to believe in their potential to do better. Student after student experienced positive results that weren't only reflected in their test scores, but also in other aspects of their lives. Coaching students felt so rewarding that I committed to it full-time.

Seeing the transformations among my students inspires me and propels me forward. Even though I was successful in high school and college, I can only imagine how much better my experiences would have been had I known what I teach my students—the same tools, strategies, and mindsets I will teach you in this book.

Having Fun and Feeling Good

When I was in high school preparing for the ACT and SAT, my mom told me, "I always *loved* taking standardized tests! I thought they were *fun!*" I rolled my eyes at her and reproached her for not understanding that this process was very serious and not fun *at all*. Today, I try to make this process fun—or, at least, enjoyable—for every student I coach. The irony is not lost on me.

Society often projects the message that working hard is primary, and feeling good is secondary. But that idea is flawed. To be our most productive selves and to make our greatest contributions, we must feel good while we work hard.

Think of something you enjoy doing. Now think of something you don't enjoy doing. During which activity do you feel more confident, motivated, and focused?

Feeling good isn't merely a nice state of mind; it is the key to being your best self. It facilitates all of the other feelings you want to have during your test prep.

Feeling good doesn't mean ignoring that the test is a big deal. Of course the test is a big deal. If it weren't an important step in the college admissions process, you wouldn't be preparing for it, and you certainly wouldn't be reading this book. Just remember that you can understand the test's importance without letting this understanding turn into an obsession that distracts you from success. That is where feeling good comes in. The more positive you feel, the better your mood, the more energy you will have, the more focused you will be, the more you can get done. Period.

How do you feel good? The first step is establishing that feeling good is a priority for you. Next, brainstorm some activities that foster positive feelings. I will provide a few tools that I think create positivity, but it's important to find what works for you. Discover ways to charge yourself up with positive energy so that you feel good about yourself and your test prep.

Spend ten minutes a day doing something that boosts your mood. In addition to helping you feel good in the moment, small actions will likely improve how you feel far beyond the ten minutes you invest in them.

Additionally, even if you don't love everything about test prep, certain aspects of prep might be genuinely fun for you, such as the shot of endorphins from answering a difficult question correctly, the adrenaline rush of finalizing your answers before time runs out, or the satisfaction of achieving score increases. Those highs are potentially enough for you to feel positive when you sit down to do the work. Plus, the college admissions test process is about more than the test. It is about investing your time and energy toward your goals and your dreams. Even in the moments when you aren't having fun, you can feel good about that.

I'm not looking to merely help you earn a better score, though hopefully that will be a happy consequence of what we discuss here; I'm setting out to help you have a better experience in preparing for and taking the SAT or ACT. This process can be pressure-filled and overwhelming, and I hope that *Acing It!* helps you filter out the internal and external noise that distracts you from your goals. I hope this book breathes light, life, and fresh air into your jam-packed, crazy days. I hope it refocuses you and helps you connect to an inner stillness that knows exactly what your right next step is in the testing process. I hope it gives you direction and purpose, and I hope it empowers you to trust your gut (and to do enough preparation that you have a gut worth trusting). I hope that this book sparks your intellectual curiosity and gives you an inkling of how fun—yes, I said it, *fun*—the SAT and ACT process actually can be.

What's the Point?

Let's take a step back and discuss the point of the tests.

I get it. You have a lot going on. The idea of spending hours preparing for an exam in the midst of everything you already do—working toward a strong GPA, excelling at extracurriculars, and maintaining some sort of social life—can feel anywhere from preposterous to tedious to overwhelming.

Thoughts like that are, to a certain extent, natural. But they are also a form of resistance. "Resistance" refers to anything that distracts or detracts from your ability to take proactive steps toward your goals.

When facing resistance such as this, I like to apply a precept of Wayne Dyer, a renowned teacher and speaker in the field of self-development. Dyer says, "When you change the way you look at things, the things you look at change." Here are some thoughts that might shift your perspective on test prep. They won't change the fact that test prep exists, but they might change the way you feel about it.

Life is filled with opportunities and challenges for which we prepare and that pass as quickly as they came. The truth is, this is hardly the last time that you will invest dozens of hours into a single morning's task. There are GMATs, MCATs, LSATs, GREs…

There are also pitch meetings, important presentations, campaigns, and major auditions, to name a few such occasions.

By fully accepting this challenge, you will develop skills and habits that help you beyond the test. Those major auditions might build on each other (maybe you don't land this specific role, but the casting director might call you in for a future role). Likewise, the skills you acquire preparing for the test also build on each other. By prepping and taking the test multiple times, each encounter becomes a learning opportunity to help you do better next time.

Furthermore, the benefits can span beyond the test. Prepping for the test can serve as an opportunity to raise your game, your efficiency, and your coping skills. By accepting life as it is right now and figuring out a way to handle it in a positive manner, you will build your mettle for the next curve ball life throws you

It isn't personal. There is a rational intention behind the tests. The goal is to objectively measure academic achievement.

The measure should be consistent whether you attend public or private school, whether you live in Alaska, Mississippi, Texas, or California. It shouldn't matter when the last time the person reading your application ate or how well rested he or she is or whether it is sunny or rainy outside when he or she cracks open your file. A 32 on the ACT is still a 32. An 1800 on the SAT is still an 1800.

Whether the SAT and ACT are the best measures to serve that role is an entirely separate question. There are organizations which are working to develop "better" systems, but the fact is the SAT and ACT are the measures currently used by those schools that require standardized tests (which is the majority of colleges).

You are choosing to take and prepare for the test. The SATs and ACTs aren't something that happen to you. They are something you engage with. Sure, it may not feel like that, but let's zoom out a bit. There are test-optional schools. There are students who don't prepare for the tests. You don't have to take a college admissions test any more than you have to prepare for it.

The fact that you are *choosing* to take and prepare for a college admissions test signifies that there are schools to which you want to apply that require the test, and that attending one of these schools means more to you than not taking the test. It shows that you are willing to invest time, effort, and energy into achieving maximum results. It indicates that you have goals, and that the SAT and ACT factor into achieving those goals. By rethinking test prep as an active choice rather than an obligation, you reclaim your power.

Here you are, faced with the challenge that is test prep. You have two options: bemoan it, or take a positive approach. Rather than struggle against the machine that is the college admissions process, I challenge you to work with it. I challenge you to lose the victim mentality and become an active participant in the process, because that's when you'll start to see progress.

Putting the Test in Perspective

One more thing before we dive into the nitty-gritty.

College admissions tests aspire to measure "college readiness." Do they do that? Not necessarily.

Any system that defines your worth by a number is an inherently flawed system. However, the process of setting a goal; taking consistent, purposeful steps toward achieving that goal; and negotiating the emotional fluctuations that arise every time you pursue a goal or creative endeavor…those experiences make you better.

As you strengthen the skills necessary for success on the SAT and ACT, you will likely begin to feel better about yourself. You will believe in yourself and your ability to improve your performance. You will improve your scores.

You will have doubts along the way. There will be times when you question your intelligence, capability, and worth. These perceptions are fluid. They can vary by the minute. One minute, everything is fine; the next, everything sucks. Scores will go up, scores will go down, scores will plateau.

Amidst all of the ups, downs, and stagnations, remember that all of this is separate from your intrinsic worth. Your intrinsic worth is not and cannot be confined or defined by a number. You are magnificent and your value is unquantifiable.

Just so we're clear.

When Should You Start?

I'm guessing that if you bought this book, you've pretty much decided that the time has come (or will soon come) to begin your test prep. You might have already taken an official test and are prepping for your next one. If any of these scenarios applies to you, you don't need my input on when to start, because you already have.

But perhaps you are ahead of the game, like I was, reading that college admissions book years before I would apply. (Reading the book didn't mean I was ready to start drafting my essays!)

For those of you who have not yet begun, these five questions will guide you as to whether now is the right time to commit to your test prep:

1. Do you have the basic academic foundation you need to be successful? This is a common concern among students, but in reality this shouldn't be a barrier to starting, particularly if you have completed your sophomore year of high school. To begin, you don't need to know everything that you will ultimately need to know to succeed. You will identify gaps in your knowledge base during the test prep process, and only upon identifying them will you be able to fill them.

Starting prep as a freshman or sophomore is probably premature if you follow the traditional academic curriculum, but you may have circumstances that make it reasonable to start prepping earlier than junior year—which brings us to Question 2.

2. Do you need extra preparation time to develop certain knowledge you don't have? When I taught SAT prep at a New York City private school where English wasn't every student's first language, I began working with students in their sophomore year so that they could have additional time working with the English-based test. I began working with another student in his sophomore year because he had learning differences and had missed a lot of basic math content during his earlier education, so we needed extra time to strengthen his math skills.

3. What are the current demands on your time? Is there a current obligation that has a specific end point? What future projects do you see on the horizon? Note: The question is not, "Do you have time?" We all have busy lives in which we juggle many different desires and responsibilities. Instead, you need to consider whether you have an objective reason to believe that you will have additional discretionary time in the not-too-distant future. On the flip side, maybe you will have new demands on your time down the line. For example, students may choose to start or intensify their prep during the summer months when they don't have the daily pressures of attending school.

Another consideration is your desired end date. Many students hope to finish their testing by the end of junior year or the beginning of senior year so that they can shift focus from admissions tests to college applications. As busy as they are during their junior year, they know that come senior year there will be new demands on their time. They want to be able to give their attention to both test prep and college applications without compromising their performance on either. While working on tests and applications simultaneously is certainly doable, it can also feel overwhelming.

4. Are you allowing yourself time to learn and grow? We often want (and maybe even expect) things to come together sooner than they do. Allowing yourself time to learn and grow gives you the opportunity to take the test without feeling like the outcome is all or nothing.

On that note, if you want to finish testing by the spring of your junior year, starting prep in the summer before or fall of junior year affords plenty of time to build a foundation, refine skills, and optimize performance. And, if you happen to finish earlier than spring? No one ever complained about succeeding too soon.

5. Does your goal feel abstract or real? You know those people who say, "The pressure is good for me?" The ones who leave studying to the night before the test or homework for 10 o'clock at night? (You might be one of them.) Part of the reason these people like working under pressure is that as the deadline approaches, their sense of the deadline's "realness" increases. This urgency-breeds-motivation mindset is why so many students up their test prep efforts in the fall of their senior year.

It isn't a bad thing that the tension accompanying a looming deadline motivates you, but you are doing yourself a disservice if you know how to self-motivate only at the eleventh hour. You can connect to the reality of your goal with or without the pressure of time by focusing on why you are prepping for the test in the first place.

Focusing on your "why"—your personal reasons for taking a college admissions test—adds fuel to your fire. Your "why" keeps you focused, motivated, and engaged with your goals and the steps that will help you achieve them. If your answers to all of the other questions add up—you have the basic knowledge; there are no extra, finite pressures on your time; you have a future obligation that will make additional demands on your time; you're allowing yourself time to learn and grow—but you don't feel motivated because the goal doesn't feel real, you likely need to spend some time connecting to your "why."

How do you connect to your "why"? That's what we will discuss in the next section.

Goal Setting, Part One

Before we discuss the logistics of what you will be doing to prepare for the test or, more importantly, how you might do it, let's talk about your personal "why" for doing it at all.

I know that the easy answer here is "because I want to go to college" or "because my parents are making me" or "because that's what you do toward the end of high school." But it's more than that —or it should be. Just as I did when I was a sixteen-year-old in South Dakota dreaming of more than her hometown could offer, you should find an image, a mantra, a desire that propels you forward. You need the *thing* that gets you to sit down and take practice tests when you'd rather be hanging out with friends or watching television or browsing the Internet—or, if you happen to be lucky enough to live near an ocean, sitting by the ocean (and who could blame you for wanting to sit near an ocean?). You need a seed of desire and you need to connect to the voice inside you that says, "Everything in my wildest dreams is possible." If everything in your wildest dreams is possible, then you have a major reason to work hard on this test: by working hard, you are bringing yourself closer to fulfilling those dreams.

Grab a notebook and brainstorm responses to the following questions:

- How do you want to feel when you attend your dream school?

- What sort of people do you want to meet?

- What do you want to learn and experience?

- What sort of contribution do you want to make to the world?

If you aren't sure, just start writing. Anything. When you are open, your heart will start speaking to you. If you are more of a visual person, draw a picture or create a collage filled with inspirational quotes and pictures of your dream college and post-college life. Dream up your destiny. That's the direction in which you are moving and where acing this test can take you.

I know it is tempting to skip this exercise and keep reading. I've read plenty of books with writing exercises that I disregarded. But I assure you, this exercise is worth your time. Pause, put the book down, and answer these questions.

Remember this exercise—maybe even review what you wrote or created—as a way to boost your motivation when you lack focus, feel discouraged, or aren't in the mood to do a practice test. There is a good reason you've set out on this journey. You aren't doing it for your parents or your teachers or the college admissions officers; you are doing it for yourself.

Ultimately, you are the only person you need to answer to, and you will know if you gave it your best shot or if you settled for less.

Goal Setting, Part Two

In the previous section, we set some big-picture intentions. Now, it's time to set some goals that more specifically relate to your test prep. Here are some of my suggestions, but I also encourage you to set a few goals of your own. Write your goals for the process down, being as specific as possible when you do. It's hard to meet a goal that you haven't clearly established. Unless you are clear and specific, the target will keep moving.

1. Learn all necessary math formulas. Whether you are taking the ACT or the SAT, it is faster to use your brain than to look up a formula on a test-provided formula sheet. You should be able to tell me the formula for the surface area of a cylinder if I were to wake you up in the middle of the night and ask you for it.

2. Learn all necessary grammar usage rules. Relating the problems to specific rules rather than simply using your mind's ear to determine what "sounds right" will help you as you move through the English and Writing sections.

3. Find a few effective learning techniques. It doesn't matter whether or not you log the hours studying if you aren't retaining the information. Using a combination of modalities is often the most effective approach to learning. It's good to experiment with different approaches, both as a way to discover productive strategies and to keep your life interesting and the methods effective. In this book, I provide a variety of useful techniques. They can be mixed and matched to engage your mind and body in different ways. If you identify techniques that work particularly well for you, you can apply them when studying for other subjects, learning lines for your school play, or remembering the names of everyone in your freshman dorm.

4. Be curious. Within the topics covered in the test, where are your weak links? As a test taker, how can you improve? This is a dynamic process, a series of experiments. Be open to each new discovery along the way. Know that every wrong answer is an opportunity to learn about the material and the best way to use your skills to succeed on the test.

5. Be consistent. Be persistent. Show up for yourself.

6. Improve your score. Yes, scores matter. Scores are the most objective indication of how your test prep is progressing. You are allowed to have off days, but track your scores, and let them serve as indicators of where you need to invest more time and energy or shake up your strategy for a specific section or the test as a whole.

You may have noticed that while I talk about score improvement, I make no mention of targeting a specific score.

At these initial stages, your focus should be on preparing— understanding the test, building your foundation, establishing good test-taking techniques, and so forth. Everything else is just a distraction. We will discuss establishing target scores in Chapter 11, and once you get to that point, you can establish a clear score goal. But in the meantime, knowing that you want to score a ___ won't change the fact that your aim when you sit down to take the test is to do the best you can with the skills you are developing.

Test Prep Options

Essentially, you have three options for test prep.

I have personal experience with each of these modalities. I prepped for my own college admissions tests independently. Currently, most of my coaching is one-on-one and with small groups of students. I have also taught prep classes at a top NYC private school.

Obviously, there are more nuanced decisions to be made. For example, if you decide to take a test prep class, will you take a class with twenty students or ten? For the most part, I will stick to exploring the broad categories.

You can certainly mix and match approaches, but time is a resource you can spend only once. Whichever method you choose, give it your all.

Prep on Your Own

This is a self-designed, self-committed program. Therefore, this category requires outside prep materials like books, flash cards, and online programs.

To use an exercise analogy, prepping on your own is like going to the gym and designing your own workout. You might use workouts published in a fitness magazine to guide you, but it's basically up to you to figure out what you are going to do and how you are going to do it (maintaining form, completing all the sets, and so forth).

Two advantages of this method are that it is the least expensive and most flexible.

However, you also miss some of the advantages of other formats. You don't have a person to bounce questions off of or to observe your test-taking technique. Having another person in the room allows an objective perspective on your work and personalized insights that you may not discover on your own.

You don't have anyone else setting the pace or directing the course of your prep. Most of the time, I don't think we crack the whip on ourselves the way an outsider does. This isn't necessarily because we are lazy or unfocused, but often we simply don't know any better.

When prepping on your own, you won't have access to as many official tests as you will within some classes or with some tutors/ coaches.

Lastly, even though the scheduling flexibility is nice, the trade-off is that you don't have anyone holding you accountable. When your class meets or you have a tutoring session scheduled, you are responsible for preparing the homework by its deadline and showing up as planned.

Ways to mitigate the drawbacks of prepping independently include setting and honoring a clear test prep schedule, finding accountability buddies with whom you can discuss your progress, and asking academic teachers for help on any topics you are having trouble mastering on your own.

Prep in a Class

In a class, you work with other students under the guidance of a teacher. I'm pretty sure you understand the classroom construct after over a decade in school. Virtual classes with interactive office hours fall into this category, too.

To return to our gym analogy, prepping in a class is akin to taking an exercise class. You have an instructor in the room with you, but you won't receive the same personal feedback that you would working with a trainer one-on-one. He or she isn't always checking your form because there's a class to lead.

The advantage is that you have a classroom of other students working on the same material as you are. Other students might ask questions that you didn't think of, but that illuminate a problem or a concept for you. You still have a schedule that holds you accountable. And, it's less expensive than one-on-one prep.

There are several disadvantages. There's a bigger chance of either feeling behind or bored. A class has a set curriculum designed for a general audience, not you specifically. If you are a math whiz, you will still need to spend the same amount of time on math as anyone else. If you have difficulty with reading comprehension, you may not be able to spend additional class time on it once the material has already been covered. You won't receive as much individualized feedback from your instructor. There's the least amount of scheduling flexibility. And, without the immediacy of one-on-one attention, you might have more difficulty staying focused.

Ways to minimize the drawbacks of prepping in a class include being willing to spend time outside of the classroom reviewing concepts about which you feel insecure, making a commitment to the set class times, and taking the class with a like-minded friend who is willing to help you review classwork if you have to miss a class and of whom you can ask questions.

One-on-One Prep

One-on-one prep can take place with a tutor or a coach.

To finish our exercise analogy, these are the personal trainers of the test prep realm. During your sessions, 100 percent of their focus is on you, your goals, and your efforts.

A tutor concentrates on the content of the test. He or she will encourage basic test-taking techniques and make specific recommendations to meet your individual needs.

Coaches move beyond the fundamentals of test preparation. They help you develop approaches to overcome challenges like anxiety that threaten to undermine your preparation and your performance on test day. The lessons you learn with a coach—such as how to effectively set and pursue goals, face challenges, and handle stress—carry over to other areas of your life. The story I told about Jamie's raising her scores while building self-confidence is a good illustration of the benefits that come from working with a coach.

For simplicity, I will group tutors and coaches together for the remainder of the book, simply referring to them as tutors. All coaches tutor. Not all tutors coach.

The advantages of one-on-one prep are many. You have all of the resources of a class (maybe more), plus you have individualized attention. The prep lasts as long as you need it. It moves as quickly or as slowly as you require. You can choose a tutor whose personality jibes with yours as opposed to working with a randomly assigned classroom teacher. You have someone specific to bounce ideas off of and to cheer you on.

The main disadvantage of one-on-one prep is the higher cost (relative to the alternatives). As with anything, you get out of it what you put into it—the more you dedicate yourself to the sessions, the sooner progress will come; the sooner progress comes, the fewer sessions you need, and the lower the cost. Also, understand that you are not simply spending money but making an investment in something that you value.

With one-on-one prep, it's also particularly important to choose the *right* tutor. Otherwise, he or she might actually undermine your prep. The right tutor will not dampen your spirit by enabling or coddling you or by being punitive or condescending. You should work with someone with whom you feel comfortable, someone who gives you the freedom to fail and the fervor to try again. There's an element of chemistry here, too. There might not be anything wrong with the tutor—he or she may have worked wonders with your older brother or friend—but he or she might not be the right fit for you. Be discerning about whether the tutor helps you to feel more or less powerful and capable. Make sure that you like your tutor and look forward to your sessions. When choosing a tutor, keep in mind that just because someone scored in the 99th percentile on his or her own test or graduated from a top school does not mean that he or she is a great teacher. Not everyone who can achieve can teach. They are different skills.

Self-Talk

How you talk to yourself throughout the test prep and test-taking process is important. Everyone has an internal negative voice, and odds are you will hear yours at various times throughout your SAT/ACT experience. What makes this voice especially tricky is that it often speaks in the first person, making its message easy to accept as true.

Sometimes the negative voice will talk to you about the big picture:

I'm not making enough progress. This is too hard, too confusing, too impossible. I'm working so hard and it isn't making a difference. I'm not smart enough to get it. I suck at this. I'm not really giving this my all. I must not really want this. It's never enough. I'm never enough.

Sometimes it will talk to you during a test:

I can't do that math problem—see, I really am stupid. Can't I go any faster? Bet I'm getting all of these wrong.

You need to figure out how you are going to deal with this negative voice. There is more than one way of addressing the voice, and you might use different techniques at different times.

One option is to tell that voice that you hear it, but you are going to continue anyhow. Like Beyoncé when she's having a bad hair day (she has those, right?), you won't let the voice stop you from being fabulous or getting the job done. This isn't about fighting anger with anger; it's about saying, "I am too awesome to let the negativity drag me down. I have a job to do." You hear the voice, but you recognize it for what it is—a distraction. You acknowledge that the voice is nervous, unsure, and unsteady. You understand and feel compassion for the voice. But YOU (the real you, the all-caps you) are not this voice. You need to focus on the test, so you confidently, fearlessly move on.

Remind yourself that the voice is lying. Maybe the voice is presenting some evidence that is more or less objectively true right now, such as you don't know the answer to a question or you've hit a plateau with your scores, but that doesn't mean that you are generally stupid, incompetent, unworthy, or unlovable (yes, sometimes the voice comes from a mistaken belief in one's unlovability). The more that you can connect to and foster a belief in your own goodness— the stillness beyond all the hubbub and drama of daily life—the better you will be able to recognize that what the voice is saying isn't true. You are a good person. You are doing your best. You may not understand how to solve a problem this second, but that doesn't mean that you are stupid or that you will never be able to solve it. Perhaps if you go back to the problem in five minutes you will pick up on information that you didn't see before and solve it easily. Or perhaps after reviewing the concepts that the problem is testing you will be able to solve it.

Another technique for managing negative self-talk in the context of the test is to practice preempting it with positive self-talk. When you read a question whose solution eludes you, before the negative self-talk can chime in, tell yourself, "I know the answer to this question." Then pause. For a moment, sit with the assuredness that you have the answer, or even the first step toward the answer. Look at the problem again and see what occurs to you. If you have no new insights, proceed with eliminating answer choices and take your best guess; you can revisit the question later. Keep moving along.

What's Your Story?

Much of self-talk is rooted in stories. Negative self-talk is the sudden knee-jerk reaction triggered by a specific moment, whereas stories are more generalized perceptions of yourself and how you relate to the world. We all have stories that we tell ourselves about ourselves. Some are positive: "I'm organized," "I like science," or "I feel alive when I play the drums." Some are negative: "I'm always left out," "Life is overwhelming," or "Nothing I do will ever be good enough." Whether or not you can consciously articulate your stories, they are affecting you, your emotions, the flow of your daily life, and your test prep. It's time to shine a light on them.

Reflect on the stories you tell about yourself—both positive and negative. Write a list. Circle the ones that might negatively affect your test prep or test taking.

Consider these common stories among test takers: "I'm not good at memorization," "I have bad test-taking anxiety," "I have trouble focusing," "I'm a slow reader," and "I'm bad at math."

If any of these feels true to you, can you come up with possible counter-evidence or some ways you could shift the story?

Here are some examples of ways to shift the story:

"I'm not good at memorization." Maybe you haven't yet figured out a technique that helps you memorize. I will provide a few suggestions later in the book. Try them out and see what happens!

"I have bad test-taking anxiety." The better prepared you are, and the more you are able to stay grounded and keep things in perspective, the less power test-taking anxiety will have over you.

"I have trouble focusing." Come up with a mantra that centers you. Tell yourself, "I can do this," or "I'm clear and focused." Or, when you realize your attention has drifted off, simply say, "I'm back," and bring your attention to the present moment. Feel the chair under you, feel the air in the room, take a breath, and reengage with the test material.

"I'm a slow reader." Try setting a stopwatch. Timed drills give you an objective measure of your reading pace. Shift your focus from the ambiguous goal of "I want to read faster" to a more concrete goal of "I want to read this passage in three and a half minutes." As you continue working, you will find that you don't need to read as closely as you may have thought you did to gather the information necessary to answer the questions. Because you are reading more quickly, you will have time to refer back to the passage to gather some of the details you missed, if necessary.

"I'm bad at math." In all of my coaching experiences, this is one of the most prevalent and easily disproved stories. Rarely have I met a student who is genuinely bad at math, at least at the level assessed by college admissions tests. There may be holes in your previous math training, but does that mean that you're bad at math? No, it means that you have concepts to learn and techniques to practice. Once familiar with the concepts and techniques, you can do the math—it falls right into place.

Revisit your list. Ask yourself if the stories you've circled are true. There may be instances from your past that seem to support the story, but because negative stories tend to be stated or felt in the extreme ("This always happens," "That never happens"), you can disprove them by finding counter-evidence. If there's a story that you screw everything up, think of at least one time when you succeeded. If you have difficulty coming up with counter-evidence because the story feels so true, try to introduce the possibility that the story doesn't have to be true. ("I might have experienced anxiety while taking tests in the past, but I don't have to experience anxiety while taking tests. It is possible for me to feel calm and confident while taking tests. I am ready to have a new experience.")

You've built your stories based on experiences, but now's your chance to adopt new stories and have new experiences. Your stories don't need to quickly transition to "I take tests with confidence" or "I'm awesome at math." A new story can be as simple as "I'm willing." Willing to learn, willing to grow, willing to practice, willing to explore, willing to forgive, willing to try. A story of willingness is enough.

The Test Has Already Begun

Although the test isn't scheduled for several months or weeks, the truth is that the test has already begun. Part of what the SAT and ACT test is your ability to prepare.

Think of an activity that you care about that culminates in a performance—athletic, artistic, or otherwise. You wouldn't show up on "game day" without having prepared for it, right? By the time the performance happens, you have spent hours practicing and preparing.

Furthermore, the quality of your performance will reflect the focus, consistency, determination, and skill you honed in your practices.

Show up to practice with the mindset you expect to have on test day, because it is in the preparation that you are shaping the performance you will deliver down the line.

CHAPTER 2
SCHEDULING

In this chapter, we will discuss scheduling. After all, if you're going to commit to test prep, it needs to fit into your life.

Maintaining an organized schedule takes time, but it also makes time. When you become aware of how you use your hours, you are better able to utilize them to accomplish what you desire.

You can be busy without feeling overwhelmed—let me show you how.

Schedule It In: The Why

When I started college, I traded my childhood bedroom for a dorm room and eight hour school days for three hours a day in class. Time once monopolized by teachers spoon-feeding material or assigning busywork was now time at my disposal. Once I had time to manage, I had to figure out a method to manage it. Since then, I have found that as my discretionary time decreases, my need to spend it consciously increases.

Your life is busy: school, plus extracurriculars before and after, homework, friends, test prep, sleep (sleep?). It is up to you to maximize your time or let it wash away in a sea of Facebook posts. Because time is so fleeting and, like money, you can spend it only once, it becomes all the more important to organize your time.

Scheduling creates structure. There is power in structure. Structure helps you be more efficient and more purposeful. Structure gives you the comfort of knowing that you are attending to exactly the activity that needs your attention at a given moment, and that all of the other items on your to-do list will also have a designated time. Breaks, too, become more enjoyable when you know you have time for them.

By writing down to-do's and appointments, you don't need to invest the energy in remembering them. You free up major amounts of mental space that you can then direct to the present moment.

Scheduling also helps you track what you've already committed to and gauge if you have over-committed yourself. In an extreme case, if there aren't enough hours in the day to get everything done, then you have likely taken on too much and need to reevaluate and reduce your commitments. If the obligations you have are non-negotiable, then you have to find additional moments that you can use productively, or you have to look for ways to improve your efficiency by tracking down distractions with the ferocity of a vampire slayer. After all, if blood is life and life is measured in time, distractions and vampires both suck the life right out of you.

Once you have everything scheduled and you're working (and breaking) efficiently, if some tasks remain incomplete, you can forgive yourself because you know that you did your best. You can also trust that whatever you didn't accomplish today you can tackle tomorrow. On the other hand, efficient scheduling might uncover chunks of time that are yours to use as you wish.

At this point, scheduling has become second nature to me. Energy that I invest into scheduling yields the benefit of allowing me to use all my energy more effectively for a net gain in productivity. Without a schedule, I'm a little lost at sea. Moreover, once it is in my calendar, it is a commitment that I will honor. Once I've scheduled laundry for a certain chunk of time, I know I can't meet someone for lunch unless I can conveniently reschedule laundry. If I've scheduled lunch, I won't cancel to do laundry. There is a time for everything.

Schedule It In: The How

Now that I've sold you on scheduling, let's talk about the logistics, the how.

First, we need to lay the groundwork. On whatever calendar you plan to use (these days, I primarily use my phone calendar, which syncs to my computer, but for years I used a paper agenda), fill in all of your ongoing commitments. Obviously, this includes school, but it also includes anything that is non-negotiable and that happens on a regular basis: extracurricular activities, religious activities, family dinners, your gym schedule, etc.

Next, fill in any one-off commitments that you've already made. This could be an upcoming family vacation, a doctor's appointment, or a friend's birthday party. To maintain the calendar, update it in the moment. As soon as you make a commitment to yourself or someone else, put it in your calendar so that you don't forget to add it later.

Test prep also needs to be scheduled. There will likely be unscheduled moments when you can review formulas or vocab words, but when it comes to sitting down and working for fifteen minutes or more, you need to schedule the time in your calendar.

In addition to scheduling discrete tasks in your daily schedule, maintain a to-do list for all of the miscellany to which you need to attend. Schedule time for chipping away at your to-do list. This way, you don't need to rely on luck or a spontaneous moment to follow through with to-do items that require completion. As you move through your day, when you think of something that you need to accomplish, add it to your to-do list. Knowing the item is written down takes it out of your head. You don't need to worry about forgetting it and you won't be distracted by trying to remember it. You don't even need to think about it until there is a moment when you can complete it. For example, you put "review math formulas" on your to-do list. A free moment may occur when you can spontaneously review the formulas, or you might review them in a scheduled block of time you've designated for miscellany. Either way, until you've reviewed math formulas, don't check it off your list.

Let's next consider how you might schedule a large block of time.

An important element of planning your time is estimating how long various tasks will take to accomplish. Do your best to approximate time demands in fifteen-minute increments. The SAT and ACT are timed tests, so it's easy to know how long to allot for a twenty-five-minute section. But test prep also includes tasks, such as reviewing incorrect answers, that have more uncertain completion times.

We've all had the frustration of allotting five minutes to a job that ended up taking twenty. People generally underestimate how long tasks take. Therefore, whenever possible, base your predictions on how long it took you to complete similar tasks in the past. As you begin paying attention to the length of time a given commitment takes, your estimates will improve.

When making approximations, avoid rationalizing why a task will take you less time this go-round than it did on previous attempts— you can reduce your estimates after you have demonstrated that you have become more efficient at a task. If you can't think of a similar task you completed in the past, make an intuitive guess. Err on the side of allotting too much time in your schedule.

When creating your schedule, anticipate that within a four-hour block, you will need at least a half hour of cushion time: four hours of scheduled time = 3.5 hours of work + a half hour of flexible time. This time is separate from any scheduled breaks. It is meant to accommodate instances when a task takes longer than you had predicted it would.

Say it's a Tuesday. You have school and then an after-school activity, so you will be home and ready to work at 5 pm. Start by using your homework tracker and to-do list to itemize everything you want to get done that evening. Next to each activity, write down an estimate of how much time you will need to complete each item. Then, make yourself a timetable using regular lined notebook paper. Give each hour four lines, and mark the time on the hour. Fill in the timetable with each activity to create a schedule, and give yourself a cushion to accommodate for tasks taking longer than expected. This

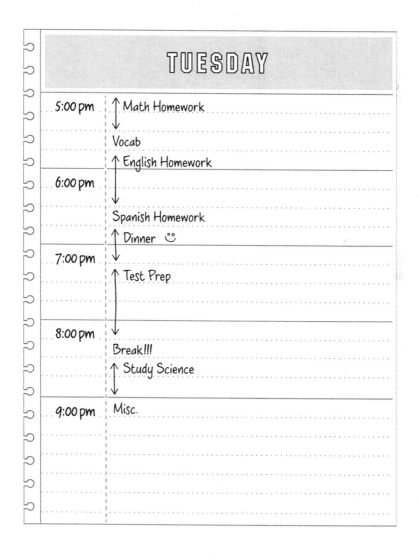

whole process should take you five minutes or less, but it will organize your whole evening.

Before we move on, there's one more important "how" when it comes to keeping and sticking to a schedule: minimizing interruptions and distractions. To find time for your test prep and your other priorities, you need to be mindful of how you spend your time and direct your energy.

The time taken by individual interruptions—whether visiting a website for fun or checking your cell phone when it chimes—may seem innocuous. But cumulatively, these small distractions quickly compound to take significant chunks of time. You could easily lose an hour to these phantom time drains over the course of an evening. It also takes time to reorient yourself within a task after directing your attention elsewhere.

When using your computer for homework, use software to block websites that might distract you; to find one that works with your computer, google "website blocker." Put your phone on silent—or turn it off, or put it in the other room!—so that you aren't distracted by incoming emails and text messages while you work on homework or test prep. If you are using your phone as a timer during a practice section, switch it to airplane mode.

Scheduling Breaks

As important as it is that you honor your test prep schedule, it is also important that you find time to relax. This requires building time for *you* into your schedule. Breaks allow you to retain information. They give the subconscious space to do its thing. Most of all, breaks balance you out and help you stay connected to who you are and what you want. If you are constantly doing, constantly stimulated, constantly engaging, it is easy to lose your center. Like other items on your to-do list, relaxation time should be scheduled in and regarded as non-negotiable. But this to-do item is a means to its own end:

feeling good.

The idea of structured relaxation time—time that you have set aside for relaxing—may sound counterintuitive if your usual idea of relaxation includes boundless time spent doing "whatever." In actuality, there are distinct advantages to scheduled breaks. Scheduling a break gives you full permission to step away from your list of other obligations. There's nowhere else you need to be and nothing else you need to do for that time. Scheduling relaxation time also ensures that you will have it, just like you schedule test prep time to make sure you have that. If you don't reserve the time, it's easy to let all of the other tasks you need to accomplish consume your time. You advance from one job to another, as if on autopilot. But non-productive time is essential to maintaining your equilibrium, and if you lose your equilibrium, your productivity and efficacy will suffer—not to mention your mood and general state of well-being. Additionally, because the time is reserved in your schedule, you can look forward to it while focusing on the tasks you need to complete prior to your break. Scheduled breaks also have a clear end point, so set an alarm to make sure you respect that boundary and enjoy your break while it lasts.

Contrast this with unscheduled breaks, which often manifest as procrastination. Unless you've already completed everything on your to-do list, you will likely feel a sense of guilt and stress. In the back of your mind, you'll think you should be working on one of your unfinished projects. Or, you lose track of time and end up rushing through your work or staying up super late. This can turn into a vicious cycle in which you're too tired to work, so you take a break, but then because you took a break you have to stay up longer, which makes you more tired. We've all been there, and it isn't fun or refreshing. It's exhausting.

Your breaks don't need to be of any specific duration: sometimes you will have the luxury of an hour or two, other times a half hour or twenty minutes, other times five to ten minutes. It's all good. You can turn on music and dance, take a nap, read a book, write in your journal, or go for a walk. Even if you just take a moment to pause, take a breath, and let yourself simply be, it will help.

Because the goal of relaxation time is to recharge and refresh your energy, try different relaxation activities. To become more aware of how a given activity affects your energy, try this: Both before and after your break, rate your energy level on a scale of 1 to 10. It is not necessary to write this down; just make a mental note. You'll begin to notice which activities help you to feel your best; those are the ones you want to do regularly.

Consistency Is Key

The more days you invest time in your prep work, the better. Never use limited time as an excuse to do nothing. You can put any amount of time to good use, even if it's only fifteen minutes at home or five minutes in the car (in the passenger seat of the car—no standardized test score is worth risking a car accident). Ideally, every day you will do something to advance your test prep: reviewing formulas or vocab, or answering a question of the day.

But your best score isn't built on mini-prep sessions alone. In addition, set aside at least an hour, three or four days a week, to do more substantial prep work. Each section requires at least twenty-five minutes to complete (thirty-five minutes for an ACT section). Most prep days it's good to spend more time than that so you can do at least two sections. You should also schedule some four-hour blocks of time in which you can complete a full practice test from beginning to end—we'll talk more about full practice tests in Chapter 6.

When I coach students, I find the best results come when I meet with a student twice a week for two hours and the student completes prep homework on the days between our sessions together. Let this serve as a guide in scheduling your own prep work.

Balance

Oh, balance. It is one of the most elusive goals in human existence. It's like a moving target. We want it all: time with our friends, time with our loved ones, time to do the activities we enjoy, time to eat, time to sleep, time to exercise, time to dance, time to rest, time to watch television, time to read (for fun), time to laugh at funny animal videos on the Internet, time to play with our pets in the living room, time to learn things purely because the topic interests us, time to explore our passions, time to fulfill our obligations—okay, maybe obligations aren't on our dream to-do lists, but today's obligations may lay the groundwork for tomorrow's opportunities. Not to mention time to rock climb, surf, go to concerts, travel to exotic destinations, and hike up a mountain at sunrise (those are on your list, too, right?).

Wanting time for all of this is great. But it's also important to become aware of your priorities. By becoming aware of what you want to spend time on, you become more informed of your priorities. If you were to wake up on a weekend day with absolutely no obligations, what would you do with your time? How much of that can you incorporate into your daily life? You might realize that when your life is busy, you don't need to do everything on your dream to-do list in order to feel balanced. You might see that you don't need two hours to do an activity you enjoy—you can feel satisfied doing it for twenty minutes for now, until other obligations ease up.

There is a saying, "You can have it all, but you can't necessarily have it all at once." Sometimes, we need to give a disproportionate amount of attention to one area of our lives. You can see this clearly if you consider your academic study schedule. When you know you have a test coming up in a given class, you spend more time on that class than you do on your other classes, even if preparing for that class usually isn't time intensive. The same is true in broader areas of your life. There will be periods when you spend more time exercising, socializing, or focusing on school.

If you start to feel like you are giving more time to one area of your life (like school and test prep) than would ordinarily feel balanced, but the time you are investing is in alignment with your broader goals, it's appropriate to tell yourself, "This too shall pass." You'll be available to attend Friday-night movies again soon enough. Right now, dedicate yourself to the actions that facilitate the life goals you came up with at the beginning of the book. Those goals are important, which makes test prep important.

On the other hand, if you feel like your test prep is taking over your life to the extent that you are compromising other areas that can't bend anymore without snapping, then take a night off. Give yourself the gift of balance. Let yourself see the friend you haven't hung out with outside of school for three weeks. Go to see the movie that looked like a lot of fun. Relax. You've been working hard. One night off won't undermine that. If anything, it will help you feel more energized when you return to your prep books.

It All Never/Always Gets Done

During college, in a given week, I sometimes had two papers due and a test looming. "It all always gets done" echoed in my mind as I walked from class to the cafeteria. As I repeated this mantra, I began to feel more grounded and more trusting in myself and my abilities. Time ceased to feel like a force working against my ability to accomplish tasks. Rather, it felt like a current carrying me along. One way or another, time would keep moving, and I would finish everything I set out to complete.

My belief in my capacity to effectively meet deadlines didn't happen on its own. It came through years of practice managing my schedule while challenging myself in school and extracurriculars. You can't sit back and watch television as magical elves write your History paper and program 5,000 vocabulary words into your brain. But you can practice staying organized and taking consistent actions. If you don't feel like you have those skills already, you can develop them. They are learned habits.

So, it all always gets done. Or, rather, everything of importance gets done. If it doesn't get done, it probably isn't important enough to matter in six months.

On the other hand, it all never gets done. Your to-do list will never be empty. As you check off completed tasks and projects, you add new ones. There will always be something you can or should put your energy toward.

In the same way that you shouldn't wait for an empty to-do list to take a break, don't wait for an empty to-do list to feel a sense of peace and confidence in your capacity to complete the tasks that you set out to accomplish. By putting forth consistent, diligent effort, you will complete everything required of you.

CHAPTER 3

GET TO WORK

If you're feeling ready to crack open a test book, then get excited. Your moment has come.

In this chapter, I will give you the overall plan for your test prep and introduce the two tests in greater detail. From there, you will take a diagnostic and choose which test you will prepare to take.

Once you've selected a test, you will procure the right tools for your test prep toolbox and start building your knowledge base.

What's the Plan?

Whenever you approach a project, it's good to have a basic sense of the steps you will take to complete it. This is not to say that you won't change or refine your plan as you progress, but having a general course of action will help you transform what might seem like a giant project into smaller, more manageable steps and clear checkpoints at which you can reassess your progress.

Here's a broad-strokes plan for your test prep:

1. Choose a test.

2. Build a strong foundation using study guides.

3. Gather data about your ability to use your knowledge and apply skills through drills and practice sections.

4. Build endurance and gather additional data by taking full practice tests using official materials.

5. Take the official test.

6. Enjoy a weeklong break.

7. Continue steps 3 and 4 as you await your scores in anticipation of the next test date.

8. Repeat steps 3 through 5 if you choose to take the test again.

9. Decide you are happy with your scores and move on with your life.

Now, let's get to it!

Choosing a Test

This section introduces the two tests and points out the major differences between them. If you are already familiar with the two tests and know which one you are preparing for, you may skim this section.

The SAT and ACT are different but interchangeable. Colleges give them exactly the same weight when considering applicants. One isn't regarded as the "harder" test or the "better" test. They are simply different tests. Because of their differences, some students are better suited to one than the other. As a college applicant, you should take the test that will help you earn the higher score. I recommend choosing to prepare for one test or the other rather than both because the more time you can spend with one test, the more comfortable you will be with it and the better you're likely to perform. Choosing one test will streamline your process and maximize the effort you put toward the test you select.

The best way to know which test better fits you and your thinking style is to experiment with both by taking one full practice test of each. Before you take these diagnostic tests, read the rest of this section to recognize some of the differences between them.

The SAT will be changing in the spring of 2016. This section describes the SAT as it has been, not as it will be.

Format

Think of the SAT as a series of sprints and the ACT as a series of 5Ks.

The SAT consists of ten shorter sections, including an essay. No section is longer than twenty-five minutes. There are three categories of multiple-choice sections: Critical Reading, Math, and Writing.

The ACT consists of four sections: English, Math, Reading Comprehension, and Science Reasoning. The ACT also offers a supplemental essay section called the Writing Test that you should plan to take because many colleges require it. The English section is forty-five minutes, the Math is sixty minutes, the Reading Comprehension and Science Reasoning sections are each thirty-five minutes, and the Writing Test is thirty minutes.

The SAT's format might work better for you if you find self-pacing challenging. If you lose track of time in one section, it won't affect your performance in subsequent sections. Because the SAT is divided into more sections, there are more restarts. Compare it to a financial budget: If you receive all your money for the year in January and have spent it all by September, you won't be in a good position for October, November, or December. But if you budget by the month, and in February you spend all of your money three-quarters of the way through, you will have a rough week at the end of the month, but you will have your full allotted funds in March.

Of course, time management, like maintaining a budget, is a practice you can learn. If you do the time drills that I recommend and keep an eye on your watch while taking the tests, you should be able to skillfully manage your time. It shouldn't take you until the end of any section, in either test, to find out that you are running behind and need to speed up.

Because the shorter sections of the SAT switch between subjects, the SAT also demands a certain amount of mental agility. You need to repeatedly jump from reading comprehension to math to grammar and back. And, because the sections are shorter, by the time you gain momentum in a section, time may be up.

Scoring

While each test is evaluated using a unique scoring system, the differences in the scoring should not factor into your choice of test.

The SAT is scored on a 2400-point scale (three sections worth 800 points each, summed) and the ACT is scored on a 36-point scale (four sections worth 36 points each, averaged). Colleges have a conversion formula that makes the two scores comparable.

The SAT employs a guessing penalty and the ACT does not. The guessing penalty refers to the quarter of a point deducted from your raw score every time you answer a question incorrectly on the SAT. No points are deducted for questions that you do not answer. The term "guessing penalty" stems from the idea that the quarter-point deduction acts as a deterrent to random guessing. The only area of the SAT that does not use this scoring system is the grid-in portion of the Math section. In this subsection (discussed below under the "Math" heading), no points are taken off for wrong answers.

The other main scoring difference regards the essay. On the SAT score report, essay performance is stated as a standalone score, but it also factors into the overall 800-point Writing section score. On the ACT score report, the standalone essay score is listed, but it does not impact the 36-point English section score.

Critical Reading vs. Reading Comprehension

There are a few key differences between the SAT's Critical Reading section and the ACT's Reading Comprehension section.

First, and perhaps most pronounced, each Critical Reading section in the SAT begins with a series of sentence-completion vocabulary questions. The ACT Reading Comprehension section may have questions that relate to vocabulary, but they are always vocabulary-in-context questions about the meaning of words used in a reading comprehension passage.

Second, the SAT Critical Reading passages vary in length (short, medium, long), and in two of the sections you are given two passages that are connected and asked questions about each of the passages individually as well as questions about how they relate to each other. All four of the ACT Reading Comprehension passages are comparable in length—combined, they are approximately the equivalent of four long SAT Critical Reading passages. None of the ACT passages relates to the others.

Third, the order of the questions in the SAT corresponds to the order in which information is presented within the passage. There is no set order for the ACT questions, so the first question might relate to content at the end of the passage, and the last question might be about a point raised in the beginning. This difference might affect how you approach the respective test's passages and questions.

Math

There are three main differences between the Math sections. The first is in the question styles. The SAT Math section tends to be more of a logic test, requiring more extrapolation from the basic concepts to solve the problems. The ACT Math section, while also including some quantitative reasoning and word problems, tends to be a little more straightforward in the way it tests math.

The second difference is that the ACT covers math content through Trigonometry, whereas the SAT tests through Geometry/Algebra II. That said, the Trigonometry in the ACT tends to be straightforward and easy to learn. Plus, you may have to study it if you choose to take a Math Subject Test down the line.

The third difference is that the SAT includes a grid-in section, for which the test does not provide multiple-choice answers. You literally grid-in the numerical value of your answer on the answer sheet. This means that if you make a careless mistake as you are solving a problem, there's no easy "tell" because you can't say to yourself, "Wait—482.667 isn't an answer choice; I must have made a mistake!"

There is an additional difference, but I regard it as a moot point: the SAT includes a formula sheet, whereas the ACT does not. Why is that irrelevant? Because you should know the formulas, regardless of which test you take. You don't want to spend precious time looking up formulas when you could have them easily accessible in that beautiful brain of yours. Moreover, by knowing the formulas, you will be able to make connections that help you solve the problems. For example, if you are told that a circle has an area of 36π cm^2 ($A = \pi r^2$) and asked to find the circumference ($C = 2\pi r$), knowing that both formulas involve the radius, you know that you can use the area to find the radius (6 cm) and plug this value into the circumference equation. Knowing the area formula triggers your recognition of the radius, which triggers your calculation of the circumference. This is a basic illustration, but it demonstrates the kind of inference that you can make when you have assimilated the formulas.

Writing vs. English

The main difference between the SAT's Writing section and the ACT's English section is in the format.

The SAT Writing section has a mix of question styles:

- Error Identification: Identify the error in a sentence or that there are no errors

- Sentence Error Correction: Read a sentence and correct the error within the sentence

- Editing in Context: Answer questions directly related to a passage and usually focused on "rhetorical skills" (transitions, rewrites, inserting/deleting, etc.)

All of the ACT English questions relate to longish passages. You are either correcting/identifying errors or answering rhetorical skills questions as you move through the passages.

Essay

The main difference between the Essay sections is in the prompt. The SAT essay question tends to be about a broad idea (for example, "Does diversity breed acceptance?"), whereas the ACT tends to ask a policy question relevant to high school students (for example, "Should schools allow students to eat food from outside of the cafeteria at lunch?"). In either case, you need to create an argument and articulately, clearly, and cogently support your argument in a well-organized essay.

ACT Science Reasoning

Lastly, the ACT has a Science section. There's nothing analogous to it on the SAT. Regardless of how you feel about Chemistry class, the idea of a Science section should not deter you from taking the ACT. Perhaps this section would be more aptly named "Data Analysis" or "Chart Comprehension," because it is less about your scientific knowledge than your ability to answer questions about the information presented in charts, tables, and graphs. Many of the questions are straightforward, so long as you don't let the scientific jargon bog you down. It doesn't matter if you know how to pronounce *Pseudomonas aeruginosa*, only that you can identify it in the answer choice having seen it written in the chart. On the other hand, if you realize upon taking your diagnostic ACT that you do not like the Science section and have absolutely zero interest in working to improve your performance on it, the Science section might be a reason you choose the SAT over the ACT.

Score Choice

Both the ACT and the SAT offer Score Choice. This means that colleges only see the score reports from the specific test dates that you select. Score Choice does not allow you to select section-specific scores from a given test date you want to submit. For example, if you scored a 36 in the Math section the first time you took the ACT, but bombed the Reading section, you can't send a college the Math score without the admissions committee also seeing the Reading score. But the ability to choose which day's scores you submit can be incredibly freeing, especially for those who have testing anxiety. Because colleges won't see a given day's scores unless you decide that you want them to, you have the freedom to fail. It won't be the end of the world if you simply try again on a future test date. With that weight off your shoulders, you can focus on the task at hand, which is to take the test one question at a time.

One caveat: Some colleges ask that you send all of your scores. There is nothing on the score report that indicates whether or not you used Score Choice, but could the admissions committee find out you used it? Possibly. If you don't use Score Choice, there's still no need to worry about lower scores, because many colleges employ Super Scoring.

Super Scoring

Super Scoring is a process by which colleges identify your highest score for each section from among all of the tests you've taken, and combine the separate scores to make a "super score." If you earned your highest Critical Reading score on the October SAT test, your highest Math score on the January test, and your highest Writing score on the May test, those would be the scores colleges use in evaluating your application, regardless of the fact that you earned the three scores on three different test dates.

As mentioned in the Score Choice discussion, admissions officers see a full score report from each test day, so it's important to do your best in every section rather than focusing during some sections and coasting through others. Admissions officers wouldn't see the 730 you scored in the October SAT's Math section without also seeing the 300 you scored in Critical Reading that day. Also, it would look strange if they noted a huge discrepancy in your various scores from one test date to the next. Furthermore, every test, every section, every question is an opportunity to practice your skills. If you half-ass your efforts, you won't receive the full benefits of that practice. Not to mention you are needlessly forfeiting the chance to earn a score that you would want to use toward admissions.

See for Yourself

Take a full practice test of the SAT and the ACT using *official* testing material. Each test's website provides a PDF of a sample test that you can download for your diagnostic, so you don't need to invest in a prep book for a test you won't take. Taking a diagnostic establishes your baseline scores and gives you a sense of which test you prefer.

Because the tests are quite long, take the two diagnostics on separate days.

When I work with students, I consider their preferences as learners and test takers when helping them choose one test over the other. You might prefer a straightforward approach to choosing a test, in which case you should simply score the tests and move forward with the test on which you scored better (compare your scores by converting your scaled scores to percentiles). If your scores are comparable, go with the one you liked better or, if you have no preference, flip a coin.

If you want to try a more nuanced approach, I'm going to talk you through an approximation of how I guide students in choosing which test they will take. This approach includes some questions that should be answered before scoring either test. Wait to score the tests until after you've answered the questions so that your responses aren't influenced by your scores.

Immediately after you take *each* test, write down your answers to these questions:

1. How did you feel during each section? (ACT: English, Math, Reading Comprehension, Science Reasoning, Essay) (SAT: Math, Critical Reading, Writing, Essay)

2. Did you finish early on any sections? Did you run out of time on any sections?

3. How did you feel within the overall flow of the test?

After taking *both* tests, but before scoring them, answer these questions:

1. Did you prefer the SAT Critical Reading or the ACT Reading Comprehension passage and question styles?

2. Did you prefer the SAT Math or the ACT Math question styles?

3. Did you prefer the SAT Writing or the ACT English question styles?

4. Do you have a gut instinct as to which test might be a better fit for you?

Next, score your tests. Calculate the scaled scores using the guidelines that came with your practice test and write down the results. Look for a percentile chart, and convert your scaled scores to percentiles. Is there a significant difference between the two percentiles (for instance, 60th percentile compared to 70th percentile)? If you felt better about the test that you scored better on, then prepare to take that test (easy!). If you felt better about the test you didn't score as well on, then look at the questions you answered incorrectly. How easily could the issues be remedied? For example, if you missed the Trigonometry questions in the ACT Math, you can easily build your knowledge in that specific area through preparation. If your scores are comparable, you can look back on your written responses to the questions about the tests and go with the test that you preferred.

That said, the most important aspect of choosing a test is reaching a decision. There's no objective right answer. If your scores are comparable and you don't have a preference, flip a coin and be done with it. Don't get so caught up in making a decision that you fail to make a decision.

Save the diagnostic test and your answers—you will refer back to them after you've reviewed your study guide.

Switching Tests

You've made your decision, but what if it wasn't the right one? Nonsense. You made a decision. Give yourself enough credit to trust that you made the right decision.

Imagine that you're dining at a restaurant. The waiter comes, and you have the option of choosing between soup or salad. You choose soup. The waiter comes with the soup, and you enjoy the first few tastes, but then you start wondering if maybe you should have ordered the salad. Maybe you can send back the soup and still get the salad. Before you know it, you've eaten half your bowl of soup and you haven't enjoyed any of it. As you finish the bowl, you alternately berate yourself for not having ordered the salad and for missing out on the soup to think about the salad. So much for that course of your meal.

You would have been better off forgetting that the salad exists. So long as you relate to the salad as an option, you split your energy. Part of you is still choosing between the soup and salad rather than making the most of eating the soup in front of you. If you realize that you've started thinking about the salad, bring your attention back to the soup.

Similarly, if you continue regarding both tests as options, every time you encounter a challenge with the test you chose, you will debate whether you should switch tests or figure out how to resolve the issue. To receive maximum results, you need to put forth maximum effort, and you can't do that when you have one foot out the door.

Should you come up against an egregious issue ("Waiter, there's a fly in my soup"), then switch. But if you are asking whether you should switch for the sake of asking, remind yourself that you've made the right choice, and rededicate yourself to making the most of that choice.

SAT Subject Tests and Test-Optional Schools

Don't become so caught up in preparing for the SAT and ACT that you forget about the Subject Tests. Colleges have different requirements for SAT Subject Tests. If the schools to which you are applying require Subject Tests in addition to the SAT or ACT, build the Subject Tests into your testing schedule.

Individual Subject Tests are offered through the College Board, the organization behind the SAT. Unlike the SAT and the ACT, which are designed to test general knowledge and cognitive skills, Subject Tests are designed to test your understanding of a specific subject. The College Board administers Subject Tests at the same time as the regular SAT. This has implications for your test-taking schedule if you have chosen to take the SAT because you can't take both the SAT and the Subject Tests on the same day. As such, an advantage to taking the ACT is that you never need to choose between taking the general test and a Subject Test on a given test day. Subject Tests are not offered every date that the SAT is offered, so pay attention when reviewing the College Board website and organizing your testing schedule.

For those Subject Tests that correspond to classes like History or Biology, it is often best to plan to take the Subject Test in the spring of the year in which you take the corresponding class—particularly if you take the AP/IB level of the class. The material will be fresh, so you can prepare by reviewing the content that you didn't study recently and taking practice tests. I also recommend taking any foreign language tests in the spring (unless you will be participating in an immersive language program over the summer), because many students don't use foreign languages as much when school isn't in session.

Consider taking the Subject Tests even if they are optional at a college to which you are applying. Your goal when applying to schools is to distinguish yourself from the herd of other applicants. If you know that you excelled in your AP English, Precalculus, Chemistry, or French class, chances are you have the capacity to do well on the respective SAT Subject Test. Why not try it and see what happens? Think of it as another way to shine in the eyes of college admissions officers.

Likewise, when applying to test-optional schools, look at the SAT or ACT as an opportunity to show your skills. After going through the test prep process, if you think that there is another way to better represent yourself and your academic abilities, go for it! I work for neither the College Board nor ACT, Inc., and my objective isn't to compel you to take either test. My goal is to help you feel and perform your best through this aspect of the college admissions process. If you want to apply exclusively to test-optional schools, and if feeling and performing well for you means not including SAT or

ACT scores, more power to you. But I wouldn't put this book down quite yet, because even if you don't end up submitting SAT and ACT scores to colleges, I think there are ideas in here that you will find useful. Additionally, I wouldn't give up on the SATs and ACTs before you've given them, as the saying goes, a "good old college try." There's nothing quite like the experience of surpassing your own expectations—and it's one worth remembering as you face future challenges in life.

The Right Tools

Before you can do the work, you need to equip yourself with the right tools; here are my suggestions for what to put in your test prep arsenal. This list is written specifically for students who are prepping independently. If you are working in a class or with a tutor, use the tools your teacher recommends.

1. Official prep books with real tests: Real tests are the Holy Grail of test prep. They are the best way to simulate the test because they are real tests. Both the College Board and ACT have released official books comprising previously administered tests for you to use in your preparation.

2. Unofficial prep books: These books dominate the test prep section of your local bookstore. They are not officially endorsed by the College Board or ACT. There are generally three kinds of books in this category:

- Prep books with study guides which review the content tested in the SAT and ACT, but contain fewer practice tests
- Books containing several practice tests with answer explanations, but no in-depth overview of the subjects
- Subject-specific study guides (for example, a book dealing specifically with the Math section)

I recommend purchasing one book from the first category. When you run out of practice material, you can buy a book that only has practice tests. If you have already worked through the study guide material in your general prep book and want additional help in a section, that's your cue to take a closer look at a subject-specific study guide.

When it comes to choosing your first unofficial prep book, skim through several prep books' study guides and see which one appeals to you. I know this sounds vague, but you need only one book with a comprehensive study guide. The material covered will be more or less consistent from one book to the next, so it is a matter of deciding which book's writing style you like.

3. Vocab lists and/or flash cards: These are only necessary if you are taking the SAT. Vocab lists may be found online by googling "SAT word lists" or "SAT vocabulary."

4. PDFs of real tests: Both the SAT and the ACT publish PDFs of official tests on their websites that you can download and print.

5. A calculator: Check the ACT and SAT websites to ensure that your calculator meets current requirements, because not all types of calculators are allowed in the testing room. Note: Cell phones are not allowed in the testing room, so don't plan to use your cell phone's calculator during the official test. Acquire a calculator you will use on test day and use it during your preparation in order to become comfortable with it.

6. A digital watch: Like practicing with the same calculator you will use on test day, it is helpful to practice with the same watch you will wear on test day—and you should wear a watch. There is no guarantee that your test room will have a clock or that you will be able to see the clock from your seat. Not to mention that reading a digital watch face is faster, easier, and more accurate than an analog clock (or watch, for that matter), which is the kind most often used in classrooms. For timing practice tests, a separate timer, in addition to your watch, will also come in handy. You can use your cell phone for this because on test day your proctor will time the sections and you will only need to reference your watch, not the phone's timer.

7. Pencils: Yep. Erasers, too.

8. A notebook

9. Index cards

Prepare to Improvise

I have a friend named Nitin. Nitin is a highly accomplished grown-up with a childlike exuberance for life. He is a well-respected neonatologist at a hospital in Brooklyn. He teaches at a top medical school. He volunteers at an art museum. He gives TED talks. And he has climbed Mount Everest. Multiple times.

When it comes to planning his trips to the Himalayas, Nitin uses the same degree of meticulousness that he applies to everything else he does. He told me once that he invests so much energy into planning because he needs to "prepare to improvise." The more attention he gives to detail during the planning process, the more easily he can adapt when things stop going according to plan. And, as you might imagine, things often stray from the plan at 30,000 feet.

Approach test prep with the mindfulness that Nitin practices. Test prep is an opportunity for you to prepare to improvise. There is no way to know exactly what questions will be on the SAT or ACT on the day that you take it. On the other hand, both exams tend to evaluate the same skills year after year, test after test. When you've gone through enough practice problems, the concepts and question styles will start to look familiar.

As you gain confidence and proficiency, you will feel secure taking things one moment at a time every time a new test is placed in front of you. Improvising allows you the freedom to make discoveries and creatively problem-solve. You don't act out of a need to get the answer, but out of an openness to finding the answer. Though you are under circumstances which many would describe as high-stakes, you feel relaxed, focused, centered, and alert. When you take things moment by moment you are, as they say, "in the zone."

Review the Study Guide, Build a Foundation

You must ensure that your foundation is solid. Your foundation is your knowledge of the concepts tested time and again by the SAT and ACT. After taking diagnostic tests and selecting the SAT or ACT, many students proceed directly to taking practice tests to build their understanding of the test. I strongly recommend that you instead shift your attention to your study guide.

There are a few reasons why following a study guide is more effective than letting missed questions direct your initial review.

Study guides facilitate learning. In a well-organized study guide, topics build on each other and related ideas are grouped together. This creates a more easy-to-follow narrative for your review than practice tests, in which questions jump from one concept to the next.

Study guides are comprehensive. This makes your review more efficient because you will encounter most (if not all) of the content covered in the test in one review of a study guide. On the other hand, when you take a few practice tests, some content will repeat and other content may not show up at all.

Study guides help you be proactive. Reviewing a study guide puts you in the powerful position of building familiarity with the topics that may arise on a test before you are actually being tested on them.

The goal is not perfection—study guide review should not be a procrastination device used to postpone taking actual practice tests. But practice tests should not replace a review of the study guide. Use your study guide to study and use your tests to test your knowledge.

Solidifying your foundation requires that you start with the basic concepts. Even if you're a straight-A student, there's a good chance that as your classes have advanced, you've lost track of some of the rudimentary terms and functions that are tested on the college admissions tests. Furthermore, the most complex questions are often rooted in the simplest operations. By having a strong grasp of the basics, you will feel more capable with not only the basic problems— you'll feel more capable with the harder problems. Start at the beginning of the math and grammar reviews in your study guide and work your way through everything.

If your study guide points out common errors, pay attention. You are not above making "common" errors. While easy to make, these mistakes are also easy to avoid. By raising your awareness of the frequently cited errors, you are less likely to slip up. This kind of mindful test taking will separate you—and your score—from the majority.

As you move through the Math study guide, take note of all of the formulas and concepts that you need to review. List them on a separate sheet of paper—you've just created your first formula sheet! (More on formula sheets later.) If you are taking the SAT, aim to learn 5–10 words a day using your vocab flash cards or word lists. Focus on words you don't already know. You may be familiar with some words in your vocabulary deck—they don't count toward your daily word goal. Review words you've learned as you progress.

Once you have reviewed your study guide, go back to the diagnostic you took and do a more in-depth review of your wrong answers. Relate the wrong answers, and any questions to which you guessed the correct answer, to the content you've been studying. Do you have a better understanding of the questions now than you did before?

Next, let's talk about how to learn all of this material.

Strategies for Learning Formulas and Vocabulary

You didn't think I'd tell you to learn all of this math and vocabulary and not give you tools to learn it, did you?

These techniques can be applied to learning all sorts of information—from names to dates to grammar rules. In this context, I will primarily discuss learning formulas and vocabulary, but once you have found study techniques that work for you, you can use them when studying many kinds of information. If you find a couple of methods that work for you and want to stick with them, great! Or keep mixing it up.

Studies on exercise show that two shorter exercise sessions in a day are more effective than one longer exercise session, and I believe the same is true for memorization. You are better off spending shorter periods of time working on formulas and vocabulary throughout the day than spending an hour all at once. Consistent review will help you take your familiarity from short-term recall to long-term understanding.

Stories

Ground a formula in a concept instead of regarding it as a random series of letters put together with arithmetic symbols. By conceptualizing a math formula instead of memorizing it by rote, you will have a stronger grasp of it. Furthermore, if you ever forget a formula you learned conceptually, you can figure it out again. Let's look at an example.

The area of a rectangle is length times width. Now, let's consider volume. Rather than memorizing "length times width times height," think of a sheet of paper. A sheet of paper measures 8.5 by 11 inches, and its thickness is practically indiscernible to the naked eye.

But once you stack several sheets on top of each other, there is an observable third dimension: height. The volume, or three-dimensional space taken up by an object, is the area of the base times the height. If the stack of paper were 3 inches tall, you would calculate the volume of the stack by multiplying the area of its base (8.5" × 11") times its height (3"). Through understanding that the volume of rectangular prisms is the area of the base times the height, we can apply the same concept to a cylinder, the volume of which would also be the area of its base (πr^2) times its height.

When learning vocabulary, make up sentences using the words. For a creative challenge, choose ten random words from the pool of words you have learned and write a short story that incorporates all of them.

In addition, it's useful to learn common prefixes, roots, and suffixes. These building blocks tell the story of a word. For example, -*ology* means "the study of." *Psychology* is the study of the *psyche*, or mind. Learning word parts will also help you make sense of unfamiliar words on test day. Most dictionaries include etymology information.

There will be times when you have to resort to rote memorization. However, when you understand the derivation of a formula or word, you will own it.

Writing It Down

A few of the subsequent techniques utilize the writing-it-down technique in different ways. But let's keep it simple: when in doubt about how to memorize material, write it down. Over and over and over and over again. Then, a little later, write it down some more. All you need is a blank piece of paper, a pen, and the information you are trying to memorize.

Cell Phone Alarms

An effective technique for learning short bits of information utilizes a cell phone alarm. Set an alarm to go off in an hour and use the text of the formula you are trying to learn as the alarm name or label. When the alarm goes off, you read the formula. Then, you create a new alarm for an hour or two later with the same text. Re-enter the formula as the label every time you create a new alarm. This provides you with reminders of the formula and forces you to repeatedly copy it down. If entering text on your phone is cumbersome, you can use the alarm as a reminder to write down the formula on paper.

Flash Cards

By putting the information you want to learn into flash card form, you are also making it easy to quiz yourself down the line. And, again, the very act of writing information down on a 3-by-5 index card is itself an act of studying. For this reason, you might want to make your own vocab flash cards in addition to, or instead of, using pre-made flash cards.

Mind Mapping

My high school AP History teacher always began class with one word written on the chalkboard. As he lectured, he added words and concepts to the board, drawing lines to connect the related ideas. By the end of class, he had created a veritable web of information that filled the chalkboard and charted out everything we covered in class that day.

It wasn't until several years later that I discovered that these crazy webs had a name: mind maps.

Mind mapping is a stream-of-consciousness way of processing information. In contrast to a traditional outline, you can easily go back and add information to an area you've already moved away from. Mind mapping is grounded in the notion that our minds don't work linearly. It is a tool supposedly used by great thinkers such as Leonardo DaVinci and Albert Einstein. If mind mapping was good enough for them, we might as well give it a go, right?

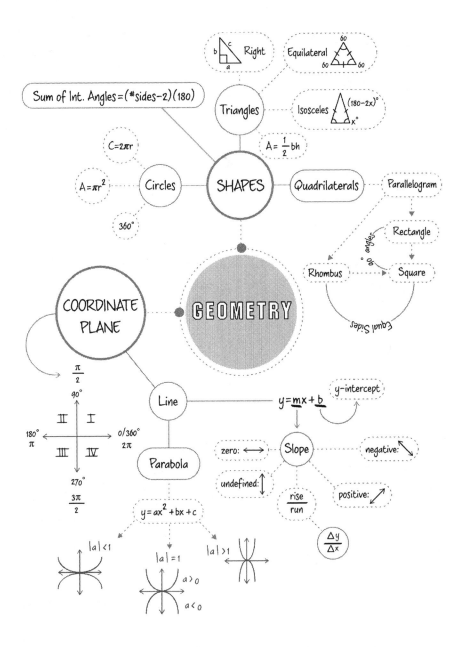

Begin with a word, picture, question, or idea, and draw a circle around it. Then write down another word, picture, or idea that the central idea triggers, and draw a circle around that and a line connecting the two circles. Repeat the process with words or ideas related to that second idea. For instance, say my first word is *Geometry*. *Geometry* might make me think of *coordinate plane* which might make me think of *line*, which might make me think of *slope*, which might make me think of $y = mx + b$, which might make me think of *y-intercept*. Then, I realize that slope also makes me think of *change in y over change in x* and *rise over run*. Then, I visualize a positive slope, which I draw, and a negative slope, which I also draw. I feel like I've pretty much covered slope at this point, but then when I look back at *coordinate plane*, I think of the four quadrants, which I draw and label, and the measures of degrees and radians, which I also draw and label. And so on and so forth, until I've pretty much exhausted *coordinate plane*.

Within the context of test prep, mind mapping can serve as a tool to find out what you know. Make a mind map around a central concept. When you are done, compare your mind map to your notes, looking for knowledge gaps and ensuring that you recalled the facts accurately. If you are still learning the information, you can create a mind map to organize the information you are studying. Mind maps can also be used when organizing your thoughts for a paper, brainstorming ideas for a project, or studying for an academic test.

Involving Your Senses

If you are an auditory learner, say information out loud. A friend of mine recently told me she says, "Off, off, off, off" as she double-checks that she's turned off all of her stove burners. If she were to simply look at the burners, after leaving the house she would doubt whether they were, in fact, off. If you love music, set a formula or a vocab word to the tune of a song. You can also use a computer or your phone to record yourself reciting a set of formulas or words and definitions. It should sound like this: "Brazen. (Short pause.) Bold. Without shame." Or, "Area of a parallelogram. (Short pause.) Base times height." Then, when replaying the recording to quiz yourself, listen to the word (or the name of the formula), press Pause, think of the definition/formula or say it out loud, press Play, listen to the definition/formula, and repeat for each item.

If you are a visual learner, use multiple colors of pens when making your formula sheet: it makes your formula sheet more attractive, differentiates among the formulas, and makes the process more fun. Find images that remind you of words on your word list. I always think of the painting *American Gothic*, which features a sullen-looking farmer and his wife, when I hear the word *dour*. You can print off or draw the pictures and paste them on notecards, putting the word and definition on the other side of the card—a fun variation on the traditional flash card.

If you are connected to your physicality, make up hand gestures for formulas. Yes, you might look ridiculous, but so what? Once you surrender to the strangeness, it becomes fun. Plus, no one is in the room with you—unless you find a friend with whom to choreograph, in which case both of you are complicit. When you know the formulas, you can let the hand gestures go. Physicality can also assist you in learning vocabulary. With friends, choose a group of 100 words, and get together once a week for a rousing game of vocab charades. So fun!

Speaking of which, you will have to excuse me. I have a vocab charade throwdown to attend.

P.S. As for the sense of smell, I've heard that the smells of mint and coffee beans stimulate your ability to think clearly!

Leverage Your Strengths

While it would be convenient if we all had a photographic memory and the ability to read at lightning speed, thankfully super-human skills are unnecessary for success on test day. Think about it: far more people score in the top percentile range of the SAT and ACT than have truly exceptional reading or math skills. But you do have strengths.

My kindergarten teacher once observed that I never sat still. Whenever she gathered her students for an activity, I would bounce from classmate to classmate to see how everyone was doing. More than two decades later, I thrive in a job that involves working with others and that doesn't require sitting still for hours at a time. This desire for stimulation and social interaction might be a liability in certain professions, but, in the context of coaching, it is one of my greatest strengths. Back in college, I did the majority of my studying in public places. Even studying by myself on a quiet floor of the library helped because there were other people nearby. Other times, I paired up with a classmate and we quizzed each other. By becoming conscious of your preferences and honoring them, you can choose tasks that work well for you—for example, when selecting a role on a group project—and find ways of doing things that leverage your strengths.

When figuring out your strengths, consider not only your learning style, but also your lifestyle. What do you enjoy doing? When have you felt successful or empowered? How can you apply these preferences to your test prep to make it enjoyable and effective? When in doubt, experiment with different ways of working.

Do your best to refrain from comparing yourself with others. This isn't about their strengths. It's about yours.

CHAPTER 4
QUESTIONS AND ANSWERS

Before we discuss the different ways to utilize the tests in your prep sessions, I want you to feel solid in working with the tests themselves.

In this chapter, we discuss the basics of approaching test questions. After all, you take every test one question at a time.

The Road to Hell Is Paved with Good Intentions

It doesn't matter if you have the best intentions in the world; it matters what you actually *do*. It doesn't matter why you got the wrong answer—perhaps you accidentally made a careless mistake, misread a question, or filled in the wrong bubble—it only matters that you answered the question incorrectly. The test doesn't evaluate if you know how to find the area of a triangle, if you understand a passage, or if you know that a comma alone cannot separate two independent clauses: it evaluates that you answer the questions correctly. Your work is not graded; your bubble sheet is. There are no points for effort, only for correct answers. All the more reason to work carefully, systematically, and precisely.

Be Specific

Be specific in how you approach each question. Ask yourself, "What concept is being tested? What is being asked? What information have I been given? What information do I need?"

Take, for example, this math question:

Montgomery Shirts is having a sale to celebrate the grand opening of their new store in the Baybridge Mall. The cost of a shirt has been reduced from $80 to $60. By what percent has the shirt been discounted?

A. 20%
B. 25%
C. 33%
D. 75%
E. 133%

"What concept is being tested?" Identifying what concept is being tested is key to starting strong as you solve questions throughout the test. In the above example, the concept being tested relates to percentages—more specifically, to calculating percent change. Specifically articulating the relevant concept will help focus your actions in solving the problem.

"What is being asked?" This question might sound basic, but it's important. In fact, of the four "Be Specific" questions, inattention to this question is the most likely path to choosing an incorrect answer. Among their answer choices, the SAT and ACT often provide options that would be the correct answer to a different question about the same information. For example, in the above math problem, some of the choices are correct answers for questions not being asked, such as what percent of the original price a shopper is spending (75%) or what percent more the shopper would have spent were the shirt not on sale (33%). They are different questions with different answers. Some may see this as the test writers' attempt to trick you, but I don't look at it that way. If you are specific about identifying and answering the precise question being asked, the options that answer other questions won't faze you.

"What information have I been given?" Gathering the information you have will help direct you to solving the problem. In the above example, you've been given the original price and the sale price.

"What information do I need?" Knowing what information you need will also direct your intermediate steps. For example, one way to calculate the percent by which the shirt has been discounted is to find the difference between the original and sale prices. You can then divide that value by the original price.

I've only discussed the questions in the context of a math problem, but they apply in other sections, too. While it may take some time at first, this process speeds up as you become more comfortable with the test and the material. Eventually, this way of analyzing questions becomes intuitive.

Reading carefully doesn't end with the question; it continues on through the answer choices. The difference between two answers in the Math section may be a decimal point. The difference between two answer choices in the English or Writing sections may be the placement of a comma. However slight, these distinctions separate the correct answer from incorrect answers.

There are no "sort of" right answers. If either the SAT or the ACT offered two correct answers to a question, their headquarters would be flooded with angry protests. Because these companies don't want to deal with irate students and parents, they have attempted to ensure that there aren't questions with ambiguous answers. If it seems like more than one answer is correct, you probably aren't recognizing a detail in the question, answer, or related passage. Time to put away the flashlight and take out the laser.

Make Your Mark

Underlining is one of the most effective ways to make sense of questions (and answers) in either standardized test. Underlining focuses your attention, helps you process information, and doesn't cost much time. When you underline text, it's as if your neurons fire and say, "Ooh! That's important. I'd better remember that." Then, when you reread a question or a passage, the key facts become easier to find.

If word problems in the Math section intimidate you, underlining helps break a given problem down into its key elements and allows the extraneous words to fade into the background. Of course, there's a balance. You want to underline key words or ideas, but you don't want to become so aggressive that you underline everything.

In math problems, you should underline:

- Key facts or figures: "Katie bought a dress for <u>$50.00</u> at <u>33% off</u> the original price..."

- Relational words: "A number is <u>5 greater</u> than <u>3 times</u> the <u>positive difference</u> between <u>6 and 12</u>."

- Important parts of the question: "What is <u>*a* + *b*</u>?"

Underlining as you work your way through passages in the Reading section is also important. Key points to underline include names (when first introduced), dates, quotations (unless there is a dialogue), and shifts in argument, subject, or tone. Within questions, always, *always* underline the "NOT" in flip-flop questions ("Which of the following statements is NOT supported by the passage?"). They've already capitalized it for you. Doesn't matter. Underline it anyway. At least half the time when my students answer a flip-flop question incorrectly, they haven't underlined "NOT." This is also true in the ACT's English section in which you fall into a pattern of looking for the grammatically correct option rather than incorrect option ("Which of the following alternatives to the underlined portion would NOT be acceptable?").

The test booklet is yours to mark up, and if you aren't underlining, you are missing out on a key to problem solving on written tests.

Show Your Work

In the Math section, clear problem solving starts with underlining, and it carries forward to showing your work: writing out the steps necessary to solve the problem. Because you use a calculator in the Math section, there is a temptation to compute the work on the screen without processing it on paper. There are a few reasons I caution against this:

- Showing your work helps you process the information. When you attempt to solve a problem using nothing more than your calculator and the chalkboard in your mind, the problem will be more confusing than it needs to be.

- It is inherently more difficult to check your work later. With nothing written down, you will need to redo the problem completely, versus reviewing your previous work on paper.

- If you guess on a problem, when you return to it, you can't see your previous attempts at solving it; when you can't see what you've tried before, you are more apt to repeat futile attempts.

- You make yourself vulnerable to calculator entry errors. Remember: your calculator does *exactly* what you tell it to do. If you input the wrong command, it will give you the wrong answer.

Sometimes, in spite of a mistake you made in processing a problem, the answer you've calculated is among the answer choices.

You will reasonably select this answer and move on. When you check your work, you can catch the mistake, but only if the work is there to read. If you haven't shown your work, you have no indication that you made an error. Furthermore, showing your work slows you down enough to decrease the likelihood of making avoidable errors.

At the other extreme, you might show too much of your work. That could be the case for you if you are completely avoiding mental math and running out of time. For example, the equation for a circle's area is πr^2. If a circle's radius is 6, that circle's area is 36π. You don't need to write down 6^2 or 6×6 if you know that 6^2 equals 36. But let's suppose you made a mistake—you read the problem wrong. The circle's *radius* wasn't 6; 6 was the measure of its diameter. A circle with a diameter of 6 has a radius of 3. Despite calculating 6^2 in your head, when you check your work you will see that you found the square of 6 rather than 3. By the way, that kind of radius/diameter mix-up is exactly why you should underline the word *radius* or *diameter*.

Just like Goldilocks, you're looking for that middle ground. You want to show your work, but not too much of it. Finding the balance between showing your work, but not to excess, is an element of your test-taking technique that you will refine as you prepare for the test.

Each section of the test has its own version of showing your work. In the English/Writing section, you might circle the noun that the pronoun replaces. In the Science Reasoning section, you might draw a line from a point to one of the axes in a graph to act as a visual guide in defining the point's value.

More Skills for Answering Questions

Most study guides deal with some or all of the techniques presented here. Many also include example questions illustrating how to use these skills. Refer to the relevant portion of your prep book and read its recommendations. I would be remiss if I didn't mention these strategies, but you likely have other resources that explain them in greater depth.

Eliminate

The most difficult questions on the SAT and ACT are within your grasp if you use the power of elimination. Sometimes, eliminating wrong answers will be so effective that you are left with only the correct answer. Other times, eliminating answer choices will be used in conjunction with educated guessing. By applying your skills and knowledge effectively, you will recognize that some of the answer choices make absolutely zero sense, so you eliminate them. Elimination will leave you with two, three, or four possibilities. By eliminating options, you've improved your odds of answering the question correctly by a significant margin. When you eliminate a choice, make a slash through the letter next to the answer, not the full answer, in case you need to refer back to the answer later.

Predict

Before you look at the answer choices, it often behooves you to predict the answer based on the question alone. Predictions can be general or specific, so long as you have a sense of what you are looking for in the answer choices. By predicting an answer before looking at the answer choices, eliminating wrong answers and recognizing correct answers becomes much easier—often, the correct answer will flat-out match your prediction.

Use the Answer Choices

Whether you are confronted by a math question with a variable or a reading question that asks you which of the following answer choices is NOT supported by the passage, sometimes the best, fastest, or only way to answer a question is to use the answers. Remember, the test booklet gives you all of the correct answers (except on the essay and the SAT's grid-in section). You need to filter out the incorrect answers, leaving you with the correct answer. We are panning for gold, people.

If you are using the answer choices in a math question where the answers are organized by increasing value, start by plugging in the middle answer choice. If you plug in answer choice C for the variable and your result is too large, you know the answer is either A or B. If answer choice C gives you a result that is too small, you know the answer is D or E. If you plug in C and you arrive at the answer you were looking for, well, you're done, aren't you?

Make the Unknown Known

This technique is useful in math questions that include variables.

In Algebra, letters or "unknowns" simply stand in for real numbers to express a relationship. To give a simple example:

Tom is hosting a party and needs 1 pizza (p) for every 3 guests (g). He has a coupon to receive an order of breadsticks (b) for every 2 pizzas purchased. How many orders of breadsticks will he receive in terms of the number of guests?

A. $b = 6g$
B. $b = g \div 6$
C. $b = 3g$
D. $b = g \div 3$
E. $b = g \div 2$

At first, this problem may intimidate you. So many unknowns! But let's get real.

Tom isn't going to invite g guests; he's going to invite 9 guests, or 18, or 300 (now that's a party). So if the SAT gave you that premise, you could plug in actual numbers to figure out the answer.

First, decide how many guests Tom is inviting. Let's say 18, since it's an easy number to work with relative to the other numbers (3 and 2 are factors of 18, so they will divide out evenly).

Then, use that number to figure out how many pizzas he is ordering, since you know that he needs 1 pizza for every 3 guests.

$$p = 18 \div 3$$
$$p = 6$$

With 18 guests, he orders 6 pizzas. Figuring out how many breadstick orders he will receive is suddenly super easy.

$$b = p \div 2$$
$$b = 6 \div 2$$
$$b = 3$$

If Tom invites 18 guests, he will receive 3 orders of breadsticks —but that isn't what they are asking here. They are asking for the number of breadsticks in terms of guests. So, now, you can take the number you chose for g, 18, and plug it into the answer choices for g. Then, see which answer choice gives you $b = 3$.

The correct answer is B:

B. $b = g \div 6$

See how when we plug in 18 for g we get the answer 3?

When you plug in 18 for g with any of the other answer choices, you don't get 3. Therefore, they are incorrect.

Two guidelines for choosing numbers: don't repeat numbers that already appear in the problem, and avoid 0 and 1—they behave differently than other numbers in certain instances; for example, any number multiplied by or divided by 1 is equal to the original number.

On the Bubble

Bubbling in your answers takes time. Use bubble sheets in your practice sessions to have an accurate sense of pacing. If you choose to redo sections of practice tests, print off the blank bubble sheet from the PDF of the diagnostic test you took and use it when retaking the test. Here are my best tips for working with your bubble sheet.

The most efficient way to fill in your bubble sheet is to work through two facing pages in your test packet and then bubble in all the answers from those pages before turning the page. This takes less time than going back and forth between the test and the bubble sheet, bubbling in each question as you go, so I recommend trying this method out a few times in practice sessions to see if it works for you. If, after practicing with it, you prefer to immediately fill in your answer choice, that's okay.

I do not recommend completing an entire section and then filling in the bubble sheet—you might run out of time and, in your haste to bubble in all of your answers, make mistakes along the way. *No bueno.*

Periodically double-check that the question number in your test packet corresponds to the line you are bubbling in on your bubble sheet. This is especially important if you are skipping problems— make sure to skip a line in your bubble sheet.

While the most egregious bubble sheet error is to fall out of sync with the test book, there is also the possibility that you accidentally bubbled in B when you meant to bubble in C. When you finish a section with time to spare, before doing anything else, check your bubble sheet, comparing the answer you bubbled in to the one you circled in your test book. I remember my mom giving me this advice when I was taking standardized tests, and it annoyed me: *I'm not stupid; I know how to fill out a bubble sheet.* But she was right. Without fail, at least once per test (if not per section) I would find an answer that I'd bubbled in incorrectly. Because I followed my mom's advice,

I caught the mistake before my answer sheet went through the machine that graded my test.

Erase your original mark completely if you need to change your answer. When you guess on a question, you can lightly shade the bubble instead of darkening it; this makes it easier to erase if you do change your answer. Just make sure to darken the bubbles before time is up!

On the SAT grid-in section, be sure to bubble in your answer below the blanks where you write your answer.

CHAPTER 5
GOOD TIMING

The SAT and ACT are timed tests, so let's talk about timing.

First, lest you think that timing is an independent variable in the test-taking process, we will discuss how building your foundation (which we talked about in Chapter 3) relates to timing. Then, we will talk about the methods and mindsets that will help you to optimize the time you have on test day.

Strong Base, Strong Pace

Many people feel concerned about pacing during the SAT and ACT. It is a real factor that you must deal with, and we are going to discuss skills for moving through the test, including exercises to work on pacing and efficiency. But I can't stress enough that when you know and understand the material—from basic facts and formulas to how you best process a Reading section—the timing element often takes care of itself.

Imagine if I asked you to spell *eudaemonic* (meaning "producing or conducive to happiness"). You'd probably have to pause before attempting it, and there's a good chance you would answer incorrectly. I'm not being patronizing here: the word *eudaemonic* was the final word in a National Spelling Bee. Now, let's say I asked you to spell the word *accomplish*. You'd likely spell it correctly and much more quickly. What's the difference? They are both ten-letter words. They are both a part of the English lexicon. Why are you so much faster and more accurate when asked to spell *accomplish* than *eudaemonic*? Easy: the word *accomplish* is more familiar to you.

The more familiar you are with the sections, questions, and topics covered on the SAT and ACT, the more quickly and accurately you will be able to solve problems. Building your foundation is the first and, perhaps, most important step to solving the timing dilemma.

Why Efficiency Is Where It's At

Whether or not you have extended time accommodations, the SAT and ACT are timed tests. The good news is that within a few hours, you're done! The bad news is that the duration of the test isn't at your discretion—the test lasts as long as it lasts, and you need to take it in the prescribed amount of time. Now, the bad news isn't really bad news; it's a constraint everyone taking the test faces. Your job is to maximize your performance within the test's limitations.

How do you maximize your performance within a finite period of time? Contrary to what you might think, it isn't simply about working faster.

Often when students accelerate their process, they answer more questions, but they also answer more questions incorrectly. They sacrifice quality in the name of quantity, and that is not the goal. Think of a computer: a computer could have the fastest processor ever, but if it were constantly freezing, deleting files, and performing actions that you didn't want it to, the computer would be useless. Alternatively, a computer that performs operations perfectly but takes ten minutes to launch a simple word-processing application isn't of much use, either. That's why we are looking for *efficiency*. You want to work as quickly as possible without sacrificing accuracy.

"Answer the questions" is a basic direction; it doesn't involve a strategy to help you maximize your score. "Answer as many questions as possible" sacrifices accuracy. "Answer as many questions correctly as possible" gives you a specific point of attention: those questions which you can answer correctly and with relative ease.

When it comes to test taking, you aren't trying to maximize the number of questions you answer; you are trying to maximize the number of questions you answer correctly.

All Time Is Not Created Equal

I sat down with Andrew for his first ACT prep session and, after a brief period of getting acquainted, I gave him a Reading section. This happened to be an ACT Reading Comprehension section, but it could just as easily have been one of the longer SAT reading passages. I asked Andrew to do the first passage in the section, and I started my stopwatch.

It took Andrew fifteen minutes to finish the questions related to the passage, and he answered eight out of ten questions correctly. As a point of reference, to finish the Reading Comprehension section of the ACT exactly on time, you need to average eight minutes and forty-five seconds per passage. Andrew was working at a pace almost half that needed to finish the section, and he wasn't even working with 100 percent accuracy.

Next, I gave Andrew eight minutes and forty-five seconds to do a second passage, and instructed him to guess at any questions he hadn't answered. In this attempt, he answered six out of ten questions correctly, but he finished on time.

This might seem like a marked difference. But consider what those 2 points would cost him over the course of a section. Andrew invested an extra six minutes on a Reading passage and earned 2 additional points, but if he worked at a pace of fifteen minutes per passage on the full test, he would have limited time to spend on the third passage and wouldn't even reach the last passage. In essence, he was throwing away as many as 20 points for an extra 4 points—hardly a good trade.

In terms of pacing, not all time is created equal. Sure, the first 30–60 seconds you spend on a math question or four minutes you spend reading a long passage are worth your time. But there is a point of diminishing returns: your initial investment is worthwhile—you must do the preliminary work on a math question or read the passage to understand the questions—but there will be a point at which spending additional time strategizing how to solve a math problem, reading a passage, or homing in on the correct answer stops helping you and starts holding you back. It's important to consider the extent to which the investment of additional time is truly benefitting your score.

Keep It Moving

Essentially, staying in flow with the test breaks down to four basic steps:

Prepare.
Believe in yourself.
Do what you can.
Let it go.

First, you prepare. As we've discussed, preparation is everything you've done prior to the moment when you sit down to do the drill, practice section, practice test, or official test. It also includes reading and understanding the question and any related material. Asking, "What is being tested here?" as we discussed in "Be Specific" may bring additional clarity.

The second step is to believe in yourself. I know it sounds hokey, but it's crucial. Believing in yourself is easy when you know exactly how to proceed in solving a problem. In fact, you don't really need to give believing in yourself much thought when you know how to proceed with a problem. But what about when you read a question and you feel a little stumped at first? That is the moment in which you need to believe in yourself. As we discussed in "Self-Talk," tell yourself, "I know the answer to this question." Then, take a breath. Reread the question, and see what insights come to you.

Next, do what you can. Take the steps that occur to you. Follow your intuition. Eliminate answer choices. You know the answer to the question is within your grasp, so proceed accordingly. I'm not in any way suggesting that the only problems worth pursuing are those to which you can immediately see a clear path to their solutions. You might only see a possible first step. See where that leads.

The final step is to let it go. In the past, it's probably felt the most satisfying to let a problem go when you've already solved it. But when you move on from a problem, you are winning, regardless of whether you are confident in your answer, because you are advancing to other problems. Feel satisfied in your ability to manage time and maximize opportunities to gain points. You know it's time to move on when you've done what you can do. Guess when necessary, and move on. By releasing a problem, you stay in flow. Any time you spend spinning your wheels is time that you aren't spending solving other problems.

Regardless of which section you are working on, there is a strong possibility that among the questions you have not yet read there are questions that you can solve easily. Some sections are not presented in order of difficulty, and the sections that are theoretically presented in order of difficulty are presented according to a subjective measure of difficulty. For example, many of the Trig problems on the ACT are quite simple as long as you know basic Trigonometry, yet they usually don't appear until around halfway through the Math section. Skipping an Algebra problem that you find challenging in favor of moving on to a straightforward Trig problem is actually more efficient.

If you keep moving, you will likely have time at the end of the section to review any questions of which you were unsure. Upon returning to the question ten minutes later, you may have new insights into the problem or see new ideas in the passage that you didn't recognize before. Your subconscious continues to work on the problem while you put your attention elsewhere. Outside of testing circumstances, how many times have you had a problem, walked away from it, and had the answer come to you while you were doing an activity that had nothing to do with the problem that had previously stumped you? It's also possible that you will come across the answer to your question in the Reading passage while looking for another answer or that a similar but slightly different question will pop up later in the test and trigger your understanding of how to solve the problem you'd previously let go. The question will be there for you to revisit. You aren't eliminating an opportunity; you are optimizing your time.

Trust that you have the capacity to solve the problem, and trust that you are doing the right thing in moving on. You aren't letting yourself down. You aren't failing. You aren't stupid. You are a savvy test taker who is maximizing the time spent answering questions correctly. This is a moment-to-moment game. It is a series of experiments in which you ask, "How might I go about solving this problem?" It's a matter of using the present moment. It's not a judgment on you or your intelligence or your test-taking ability.

In my first session with Emma, I asked her to tell me about her previous experiences taking the ACT.

When she took the ACT, she didn't recognize how to solve the fourth Math problem. Emma was an A student, and she'd worked hard on her test prep up until this point. The notion of having difficulty with the fourth Math problem seemed unforgivable. Thoughts like "I'm so stupid," "I'm such an idiot," and "I've screwed it all up" rushed through her head. Her breathing became shallow and her heart rate escalated. What's more, even once she skipped the question, the physiological effects of her anxiety lingered, and she had trouble focusing for the remainder of the section. During the break, she cried in the bathroom. In the remaining sections, she felt completely despondent.

We can all understand why having trouble on question four in a test arranged by difficulty might be a bit disconcerting. But do you know what's vastly more disconcerting? The idea of throwing away fifty-six other questions (not to mention the remaining sections) because you are so upset you didn't know how to answer the fourth question in a given moment.

If Emma had followed my method (which she did on future tests, to very positive results!) she would have taken a breath, reinforced her ability with an "I can solve this"–style thought, opened herself to insights, and, if she still didn't know what to do, she would have guessed and moved on.

Question number four will still be there five (or forty-five) minutes from now. Because it was question number four, chances are when Emma came back to it, she would have been able to solve it quite easily. And, if not, so what? She'd have answered most, if not all, of the other fifty-nine problems correctly.

When you come back to the question, have an open mind. Reread the question, underlining key information as you go, to ensure that you have not overlooked a significant piece of information. In the Math section, double-check your work. If you can't spot your error and you've used up all your workspace, try erasing your work and starting over. Among those questions that you are able to successfully solve the second time around, chances are that you simply made a computational error or misread the question or an answer during your first pass through.

Remember, you don't need a perfect raw score to merit a very good score on either test—heck, you may not even need a perfect raw score to get a *perfect* scaled score on a section, depending on the curve. If you look at a raw-to-scaled score conversion chart, you will realize that you have more room for error than you might imagine.

The advice to keep moving holds regardless of whether your goal is to score in the 70th or the 99th percentile. The main difference between how this strategy plays out in each case is how often you will feel stuck by a question. Which brings us back to step one: Prepare. Having to let go of a problem without solving it should be the exception. The content covered by the SAT and ACT is limited. Between building your foundation and reviewing practice tests, you will build skills so that as you get further along in your test prep, the number of times you have to keep it moving without confidently answering the question decreases. If you don't see that kind of progress, call on reinforcements! Ask a friend, mentor, parent, or teacher to review one of your practice sections with you. Or, talk to your parents about the possibility of bringing in a tutor to help you cultivate confidence and clarity.

The ABC(DE)s of Guessing

Test takers often feel anxious around guessing, which is why I'm going to discuss the topic with you in depth.

As you move through the test, you will read questions. Some you will solve adeptly, while you may feel less certain of others. If the latter is the case, eliminate what you can, guess, circle the question number in your test booklet as a cue to review the question during your second pass through the test, and keep moving. Don't leave a single question you read unanswered.

I'm going to expand on all of this—why to guess, why not to skip questions, and how to keep moving. First, let's discuss how the scoring policies do—and don't—impact your approach to guessing on each test.

The ACT, like most tests that you take for school, gives credit for correct answers and doesn't penalize missing or incorrect answers. Even if you're guessing randomly, there remains a 20–25 percent chance that you will earn a point for any given question. There is no reason to leave any question blank on the ACT. When you are running out of time, bubble in answers to any unanswered questions in the section, including those you haven't yet reached.

The SAT, on the other hand, has a guessing penalty. While this penalty may be intended as a deterrent to guessing, you should guess on every question you read on the SAT, too, in spite of the quarter-point deduction. Guessing when wrong answers cost you points might feel counterintuitive at first. When I was taking the SAT in high school, I followed the standard advice of only guessing on questions when I had eliminated at least one answer. After all, why would you want to risk a quarter-point deduction when you haven't the faintest idea which answer is correct? As a test prep coach, I considered the topic more deeply than I ever did as a test taker, and I came to a new conclusion. Let's take the emotions out of it and look at this with clear, objective numbers.

With five answer choices per question on the SAT, statistically speaking, by guessing randomly on five questions you would likely answer one correctly. On the other hand, you would answer four out of five questions incorrectly. As such, the scoring looks like this:

1 correct answer: +1 point
4 incorrect answers: -0.25 points × 4 = -1 point
Net gain/loss: 1 point – 1 point = 0 points

One correct answer and four incorrect answers cancel each other out. We can also demonstrate this result using statistics. To find the probable outcome, we multiply the value of each possible outcome by its respective probability:

Value of a correct answer × probability of a correct answer =
    $1 \times 0.2 = 0.2$
Value of an incorrect answer × probability of an incorrect
    answer = $-0.25 \times 0.8 = -0.2$
Probable outcome = $0.2 - 0.2 = 0$

Again, the positive outcome (answering correctly) and the negative outcome (answering incorrectly) cancel each other out. Therefore, let's rebrand the quarter-point deduction. Rather than referring to it as a guessing penalty, let's think of it as a guessing neutralizer. Statistically speaking, you have nothing to lose by guessing, even when you guess randomly.

That said, most of the time you won't be guessing randomly. Generally, by simply reading a question, you will have at least a hunch that allows you to eliminate one or more answer choices. Guessing's potential benefit to your score improves as you eliminate answers. When you eliminate merely one answer, the expected value of your score becomes a positive:

$$1 \times 0.25 = 0.25$$
$$-0.25 \times 0.75 = -0.1875$$
$$0.25 - 0.1875 = 0.0625$$

That value is quite small, but it has shifted into the positive domain, indicating a positive impact on your overall score. The expected values obviously increase as you eliminate additional answer choices. At best, a guess is worth a positive value. At worst, a guess is neutralized and has zero value. Use whatever insights are at your disposal to eliminate wrong or possibly wrong answer choices and improve your predicted score by guessing among the remaining choices.

Given that we've recognized that the guessing penalty is actually a guessing neutralizer, and the more answer choices you eliminate, the better your odds of answering correctly, your best approach to guessing is one in which you go into the test with the intention of answering every question, including those on which you have to guess. This approach has three major benefits:

- You won't spend energy or time deciding whether or not to guess. By making the decision to guess in advance, you simplify the process and remove a source of test-taking anxiety.

- You will confidently eliminate answers. As I mentioned, some people recommend that you eliminate at least one answer choice before you guess on the SAT—this is the advice I followed way back when—but that advice is without statistical support and creates unnecessary anxiety over eliminating answers. In my approach, because you've committed to answering every question you read, you are incentivized to eliminate answer choices when you don't immediately recognize the correct answer to a question. You can follow your gut. If an answer choice seems wrong, you have every reason to eliminate it.

- By filling in answers to every question, you are less likely to mess up your bubble sheet by failing to skip a line.

These probability computations do not take into account carelessness or errors in logic. Sometimes you are on the wrong track with a problem. However, more often, when you eliminate an answer choice, one of the remaining options is the right answer.

So, you won't leave questions that you've read unanswered. You are prepared to guess. But why guess right away? Why not skip the question and revisit it later?

As we've discussed, with most questions—particularly on the Critical Reading/Reading Comprehension, Writing/English, and Science sections—you will be able to easily eliminate one, two, or three answer choices. Guessing right away saves you from that awkward, panicked moment when time is running out and you have to go through and figure out which answer choices you haven't eliminated and bubble in answers from the remaining options. It's also more efficient. When you read a question and consider it, you've started the process of solving it. If you skip without guessing, you lose that train of thought and need to find your bearings again the next time through. Lastly, guessing on any section (including Math) minimizes the mistakes you may make in filling out your bubble sheet.

So, regardless of whether you are taking the SAT or the ACT, you should guess on all of the questions that you read. But what happens when you are running out of time? On the ACT, I told you to fill in random bubbles. On the SAT, the strategy is different.

In the ACT, the predicted value of a question answered through random guessing is 0.25 or 0.2, depending upon the number of answer choices in a given question. Because there is no guessing neutralizer, the predicted value is always positive. The same advantage does not carry over to the SAT, where we've seen that the predicted value of a question answered through random guessing on the SAT is zero. You have nothing to lose by filling in random bubbles, but you have nothing to gain, either. There are other actions, however, that offer something to gain with those last few minutes:

- Checking your work
- Seeing if you have new insights into questions which you previously answered with a guess
- Looking ahead for questions that you have yet to answer that you believe you could answer quickly

Choose a course of action, but do work during crunch time on the SAT—don't blindly bubble in random answers.

To be clear, the one area in which it's okay to skip without guessing is the grid-in portion of the SAT Math section. The odds of guessing correctly are practically zero. If you feel stuck in other areas of the Math section, see if there is an alternative problem-solving method like Make the Unknown Known or Use the Answer Choices that will help you to arrive at the correct answer. See if any of the answer choices appears to be flat-out unreasonable. From there, make your best guess—if there are three answer choices that are negative numbers and two that are positive, go with one of the three answers that is a negative number simply because there are more of them.

You will not always feel 100 percent confident in your answer choice. That said, the stronger your knowledge base and test-taking skills, the better your guesses will be. Become comfortable with the unknown. Don't think of guessing as a defeat, but as a part of good test-taking technique.

No Judgment

People have a natural tendency to evaluate how things are going. Constantly. Does he/she like me? Does he/she *like* like me? Is the audition going well? Is this interview going well? And, most pertinent to our discussion, is this *question* going well? Is this *test* going well?

What I'm going to advise you might be easier said than done, but I want to plant the seed anyway, because if you can master this, it will definitely help you on test day:

Don't evaluate the difficulty of a problem.

You cannot read and answer a question if you are simultaneously assessing the problem's level of difficulty, let alone the difficulty of the problems that precede it. As in any other circumstance in life, when you begin judging the test, you become an observer rather than an active participant. You divert your time and energy to judging problems rather than solving them. *Do the problem. Don't judge it.* The test is what it is, and properly evaluating how difficult it is/isn't or was/wasn't is a judgment that you can defer until after you leave the test room.

If you are having a hard time doing the problem, take your best guess and move on. As long as you are taking steps toward solving a problem, you are making progress (and maximizing the number of questions you answer correctly), so the level of difficulty of the problem you complete is irrelevant. In other instances, when you believe the test is going well, you might become careless and begin to make mindless errors.

Judging your performance and the difficulty of problems also sets you up for the rise before the fall. Some of the sections are arranged in order of difficulty—namely, both tests' Math sections, as well as the SAT's Writing section and the sentence completion component of the SAT's Critical Reading section. At first you're all, "I'm doing so well. This test isn't so hard. I must have really prepped well for this thing." Then, inevitably, you make it two-thirds of the way through the section. Suddenly, the questions become harder. You feel flustered. What happened? You were feeling so confident a few minutes ago.

You have just played out the rise before the fall. You congratulated yourself only to later experience difficulty. A complex problem escalates from being just another problem you want to solve to a burst bubble. And burst bubbles mean panic. That these sections are arranged in order of difficulty isn't news. Yet, somehow, it can take test takers by surprise.

If you stop judging the questions and your performance, you can prevent these mental and emotional swings. By not judging yourself when the test is going well, you won't judge yourself when the level of difficulty increases. Instead, moving through the test will become a natural progression. First one problem, and then another. Rather than worrying about the difficulty of a problem, you'll focus on finding its answer.

Use (all of) Your Time Wisely

While working on practice sections, you may finish in less than the regulation time. Even if it isn't your experience at this stage in your prep, as your skills improve, you will likely improve your efficiency, and possibly find yourself finishing early. If you finish under the allotted time in even one section, it is worth considering what to do with that extra time.

When you finish early during a practice section, you may be tempted to pat yourself on the back and say, "Awesome. More time for television" (or homework, sports, friends, a book...basically, anything besides standardized test prep). I know it's tempting to walk away completely or start checking your answers against the answer key, but stay strong. The section isn't over until you have used all of the allotted time. Think about it: on test day, you will have no choice but to sit until the timer has run out, no matter how early you finish. In the interval between your finishing the test and the proctor calling "time," it will be just you and the test. You need to know how you are going to deal with that downtime, and the best way to know how you are going to deal with it is to practice dealing with it.

Once you have finished your first pass, check your bubble sheet. Compare the answers you circled in the test book to what you have filled in. You should intermittently check your bubble sheet as you work, but finishing the first pass is a good checkpoint to make sure your bubble sheet accurately reflects your intended answers.

Next, review all of the questions to which you guessed the answer.

Finally, as time allows, reread every question (every single question), go through your work, and look for careless mistakes. No one realizes he or she is making a careless mistake while it's happening. Don't let your confidence turn into cockiness by believing that you are above such errors. We're all susceptible. Start at the beginning, and work your way through.

A trap many people fall into when lacking confidence—on the test and in life—is second-guessing their decisions. Second-guessing might lead you to change a correct answer to a wrong one. Avoiding this possibility is not worth sacrificing the opportunity to catch mistakes. Instead, decide that to change an answer, you should have a clear reason as to why another answer choice is better. In a moment when you think you may not have chosen the best answer, take a breath and ask yourself if you can see a flaw in your original answer or if you have a new insight that points you toward revising your choice. If either of these is the case, by all means, make a change. Otherwise, go with your first instinct.

In the NFL, the default assumption is that "the ruling on the field stands." That said, when an NFL referee makes a close call, officials sometimes review video playback. The referee in the booth needs clear evidence to reverse the call, but sometimes it happens. Even though the assumption is that the ruling stands, there's still very good reason to review close calls.

Keeping Pace

Watch technique is important for your mental clarity while working on a section. When you aren't checking your watch, it's easy to lose your sense of time and move at a pace too slow to finish, or so quick that you sacrifice accuracy. The more comfortable that you become using your watch, the more confident you will feel while working through a section. Ultimately, taking the SAT or ACT shouldn't feel like a race against the clock. Therefore, developing the ability to manage your time is an important component of strong test taking.

Simply wearing a watch isn't enough; you need to use it. Many students resist looking at their watches. Some worry about what they will see (*"Only eight minutes left! Oh no!"*); others feel they are squandering precious seconds by letting their eyes stray from the "prize." But in this case, ignorance is not bliss. To stay on pace, you need to stay conscious of how quickly time is passing. Between the pressures of the test and your focus on the questions, your subjective sense of time probably doesn't match the objective measure of time. Checking your watch throughout the test tells you if you need to accelerate (or, as we discussed previously, work more efficiently) because you've fallen behind—while you still have time to compensate. You actually risk losing time by not checking your watch. Better to find out sooner rather than later that you need to pick up the pace.

It's best to procure a test-friendly watch early on in your test prep so that when you take practice tests you can use the same watch you plan to wear on test day. As I mentioned in the section on tools in Chapter 3, I highly recommend that you wear a digital watch when taking the test. If you or a family member does not already own a digital watch, you can buy an inexpensive one. The most important feature of a test-friendly watch is a clear, easy-to-read display. Meanwhile, set a separate timer (perhaps your cell phone's timer—be sure to put your phone on airplane mode!) counting down from the total time allotted for the section you are completing. It will alert you when time is up. Place this timer face down—you won't see a countdown on test day.

When starting a section, jot down the section start and end times before you begin answering questions. You can quickly calculate the end time based on the start time and the amount of time allotted to the section. So, if I started the ACT's forty-five-minute English section at 8:10 am, I would write down 8:10 and 8:55. I might also mark 8:32 around halfway through the seventy-five-question section. Making these notes would take me approximately thirty extra seconds, but they would be thirty seconds well spent.

Keep in mind that you won't necessarily work at a constant pace throughout a section. For example, in the SAT Critical Reading section, you will move through the sentence completions more quickly than the reading passages. In each test's Math section, the problems are organized in order of increasing difficulty. Because of this variability, adjust your pacing in a way that accommodates the flow of each section. When setting pacing goals, don't forget to budget time to check your work. For example, the ACT Science Reasoning section lasts thirty-five minutes and has forty questions divided among seven passages. If you want to finish with some time remaining, you need to work at a pace of approximately four-and-a-half minutes per passage.

You might want to use your watch in chronometer (stopwatch) mode because you can start it at zero and see exactly how much time has elapsed without calculating the difference between the current time and the start time. The one problem is that most digital watches make a beeping noise, and watches that beep are not allowed in the test room. The only way that a proctor will know your watch beeps is if you press one of the buttons. But, alas, you need to press a button to start a chronometer. You can still use a chronometer mode during drills at home, but make sure you also practice using your watch the way you will use it in the test room.

Alternatively, you may buy a watch specifically designed to be used during the SAT or ACT. These watches have digital displays, don't beep, and come programmed with timers for each of the tests' sections—super handy, but if you already have a digital watch you are comfortable using, you can stick with that.

CHAPTER 6
TAKING PRACTICE TESTS

Once you've set yourself up with a solid foundation and familiarized yourself with the principals of time optimization, you're ready to move into practice tests—the best way to gauge your proficiency with the test and your ability to work under testing conditions.

If done mindfully, the more questions and passages you encounter, and the more tests you take, the better off you are. Each prep session is an opportunity to learn or to reinforce what you've already learned. Each question is an opportunity to see an idea presented in a new way. Opportunities to learn are a good thing. Take practice tests. Complete practice sections. Do drills. A lot of them.

In this section, we will discuss how to structure your prep sessions, different ways to work with the test material, how to get the most out of each session, and a good mindset to adopt when the quality of your practice session seems to be compromised.

Oh, one more thing: don't discard practice tests once you've completed them; they will provide useful material for review the week before the test.

Rationing Official Materials

It is important to ration your copies of the official tests, because you have access to a limited number of them. How quickly you go through the official practice tests depends on factors varying from how many real tests you have (for example, by purchasing the respective official prep guides, you will have ten SATs and five ACTs), how close you are to the official test date, and how many times you plan to take the official test.

For example, suppose that you are taking the ACT and you used all five practice tests from the official ACT book before your first test. You will probably be able to find a few PDFs of official tests online to help you prepare for your second test, but then you will have exhausted your materials before you take the test a third time. And, while reusing test materials serves a purpose, it's a different experience from taking a test for the first time. That said, you don't want to reserve your official tests so long that you hardly use them.

It's a tricky balance, but here's my suggestion for allocating unofficial and official test materials: after your initial diagnostic, save official materials for full practice tests. Non-official material is modeled on the official material and provides great practice when doing individual sections and drills between full tests. As your prep progresses and your confidence builds, you can start working more with official material.

If you are prepping over the summer, you'll likely want to use non-official practice tests even when you take a full practice test because you have as many as three months before you'll take the official test.

Individual Sections

You don't need to do a full test every time you sit down for test prep.

Individual sections are less time intensive than full tests, making them easier to fit into a busy day. Doing individual sections also allows you to focus your efforts. One day you might do two Math sections; another day you might do one Math section and one Reading/Critical Reading section. You might do half of a test one day and the other half the next day.

Time permitting, it's nice to proceed through your test prep by layering your work on the different sections. Begin your prep by learning the content relevant to one section of the test (for example, English/Writing or Math). Practice with only that section until you feel comfortable with it. Then, as you gain proficiency, you can add on another section and practice intently on that subject, while continuing your work on the first subject. Continue, adding one section at a time. Once you are confident in all sections, you can begin completing full tests.

Drills

Drills play with the element of time to hone specific aspects of test taking like accuracy and efficiency. Before you drill, you should have a baseline measure of your performance under timed conditions.

It's good to infuse variety into your test prep. For one, it keeps your prep interesting. For another, it allows you to target your prep to address specific skills. Basketball teams don't limit practice to scrimmaging; they also do dribbling drills. If you exclusively do practice test after practice test but never work on refining your technique, you will likely hit a plateau and never figure out how to break through.

As you move through your test prep process, switch among untimed drills, hybrid drills, timed drills, full sections under timed conditions, and full practice tests.

To complete most of these drills, you will want to use a timer in addition to your digital watch. (Remember, your digital watch should be on your wrist every single time you sit down with the test, not solely on test day.)

Untimed Drills

Untimed drills allow you to focus on your technique to improve your understanding of the test and overall accuracy. Put away your stopwatch and simply experience taking the test. Complete an entire section in a sitting so that you can sense the progression of the questions. Without the pressure of time constraints, see how answer choices in the Reading section correspond to the passages, understand how a Science passage relates information, identify which math concepts you need to review, and be especially mindful to avoid careless errors. Untimed drills are particularly useful when you are first starting out and getting to know the different sections, but don't work completely off the clock more than once or twice. On the actual test day, you will be working under timed conditions, so it's best to bring in the element of time sooner rather than later.

Hybrid Drills

Hybrid drills are an alternative to untimed drills. Work as long as you need to on a section, but use the chronometer feature on your watch or timer to track exactly how long it takes you to complete it. The advantage of a hybrid drill over an untimed drill is that even though you can take as long as you need to finish a section, you receive data about how long the section took you to complete. With this information, you can assess to what extent (if any) you went over the allotted time and how you might increase your pace while maintaining accuracy.

Timed Drills

In addition to timed full sections and full practice tests, there are four kinds of timed drills that I've found helpful in my work with students:

1. Do a full section. As you work through the section, record how much time has elapsed when you are 25 percent, 50 percent, 75 percent, and 100 percent finished with the section (percentage based on the number of questions in a test). Or, if the section is organized into passages, mark down how much time has elapsed after each passage. Put marks in the test book at each checkpoint as a reminder to note how much time has elapsed. This is a great way to track where your time goes. Did you work at a consistent pace? Did you let yourself dwell on one question or passage, costing you time?

2. Give yourself a set amount of time (for example: ten, fifteen, or twenty minutes). Work as efficiently as you can, and see how many problems you can answer correctly in that time. You can start anywhere you'd like within a section. In a Math section, you can also start at the end with the most difficult problems and work backwards. Note that where you are working in a section may affect your pace: you will probably answer more questions in a given amount of time if you start at the beginning of a Math section than you will if you start at the end. Where you choose to start depends on your objective. Some students I've worked with want to raise their ACT Math scores from a 31 to a 34, so I've assigned timed drills in which they start at the end of a section and work backwards for fifteen minutes. This strategy focuses the students on the most difficult problems in the section. If a student has trouble with careless mistakes, I might have the student start at the beginning of a Math section, because working accurately in the beginning lays the groundwork for working accurately throughout the test.

3. Time yourself as you answer a set number of questions in an SAT or ACT section or as you complete a passage within an

ACT English, Reading Comprehension, or Science Reasoning section. Again, the goal is to increase pace while maintaining accuracy.

4. Time yourself doing a set number of questions in a set amount of time. Think of this as an abbreviated section in which you are specifically trying to complete the problems at the pace you would need to move to finish the section. If you are running out of time, proceed as you would at the end of a section—either random guessing or doing some sort of active work, depending on your test. If you finish early, go back and check your work within the problem set.

Full Practice Tests

To simulate test day, take a full practice test.

Taking a full practice test is analogous to the dress rehearsal for a play. Before dress rehearsals, the company has rehearsed and done a dry run, but something qualitatively different happens when the production adds lighting, props, set changes, costumes, and makeup. Two or three times before you take the test, you should wake up early on a Saturday, eat breakfast, go to the public library, and take a full test using regulation time. These are your dress rehearsals. Schedule them into your calendar.

There are a number of reasons why you should take a full practice test in one sitting, but the biggest reason is endurance. Most students rarely sit and take a test for four hours (or longer, if you are working with extended time accommodations). Even in school, when students theoretically work for eight hours a day, there are opportunities to stand, stretch, chat, and shake off whatever happened in the previous class. In a college admissions test, you move directly from one section to the next, with only one break. You need to build endurance so that test-taking fatigue doesn't undermine your efforts.

You'd be surprised what a dramatic effect fatigue can have on your scores. Sections that didn't pose a significant challenge when taken individually can feel difficult when taken in an extended testing session. Or maybe you run out of time where you've always had time to spare. Or you start making careless mistakes. There are many symptoms of test-taking fatigue; to minimize them, you need to practice taking the test in a single practice session.

Taking full practice tests helps increase your stamina. A smart 5K runner would never attempt to run a full marathon without building to longer distances, and you shouldn't expect to perform as well on a full practice test as you do on practice sections without building endurance. Taking a test for four hours straight is hard, and that's why smart test takers practice working for an extended period before test day.

If you have less than a month before your first official test, taking two full practice tests on Saturday mornings leading up to the test may not be feasible, but try to ensure that you can do at least one Saturday-morning test simulation. If you can, do a second full practice test, even if it isn't on a Saturday morning.

You might also consider inviting a few friends to join you in taking a practice test (working individually, of course). By including others in your mock test, you will gain the experience of having other people in the room, you will be held accountable to show up for the practice test, and you won't feel like your ACT/SAT prep is causing you to "miss the party." Heck, this way, your ACT/SAT prep is the party. Between practice test sessions and vocab charades, people will be like, "Wow. You throw the best parties *everrr!*"

Other Ways to Build Skills

Picture It

Once you've found the solution to a question you answered

incorrectly, use your phone to take a picture of the question and the work you did to solve the question. Add the photo to an album containing images of challenging test prep problems. When you have downtime, review the album. This exercise isn't practical for questions pertaining to Reading/Critical Reading passages, but can be very helpful in building skills for other test sections.

Thinking Out Loud

Verbalize your train of thought as you complete a problem set for the first time. When you think out loud while solving problems, you can see where you get stuck in the problem solving. If you are stuck for too long, that's a sign to guess on that problem in order to maintain your problem-solving momentum.

Redo Old Problem Sets

Try redoing a section you completed a few weeks or months ago. Sure, some of the problems may look or feel familiar, but that's okay. This time around, can you identify which grammar rule to apply to a question that stumped you on your first attempt? Do you see how to solve that math problem a little more quickly? Awesome. That means you are learning. Of course, this won't tell you how you will perform on new material—you need new material to figure that out.

If you want to redo old problem sets or if you think you might want to do so later, it will work best with either PDFs that you can reprint or clean prep books. If you plan to use prep books, you may want to either show your work on a separate sheet of paper the first time you take the test so that the original book remains clear of markings or buy a new copy before redoing the section.

Categorize Problems

Go through a previously completed section, asking yourself, "What concept is being tested?" In the margins of the test, write down the basis of each question, being as specific as possible. Some questions will deal with more than one topic.

In this exercise, you repeatedly and purposefully perform the first step of problem solving: identifying the core topic. As soon as you know what, precisely, is being tested, the entire problem becomes much clearer and less confusing.

Even if you are only able to identify "triangles" as the topic, you have a frame of reference that you can use to narrow down to an even more specific frame of reference. For example, is it a right triangle question? Is it a Trigonometry question or a Pythagorean Theorem question? Or, perhaps, is it a special right triangle (triangles with angles measuring 45-45-90 or 30-60-90) or Pythagorean triple question?

Once you've written down the core concept to which each question relates, you can return to the section in the future when you want practice with a given topic.

This exercise is particularly helpful with Math and English/ Writing.

Repepepepetition

Let's say that you have a basic understanding of a topic but are, nonetheless, feeling stressed or answering questions incorrectly when that topic comes up on a test (and you know what topic is being tested because you've been asking "What concept is being tested?" when going through a test). How do you reinforce your skills? Practice.

If you are having trouble factoring, practice factoring. If you are having trouble keeping surface area and volume straight, do a bunch of surface area and volume questions—particularly word problems that require you to distinguish whether the question can be answered by finding the surface area or the volume.

Once you've used up all of the review materials in your study guide, you can find worksheets online by searching "[topic] worksheet" or "[topic] pdf" (for example, "simplifying radical expressions worksheet"). You can also search for worksheets related to grammar topics, such as "its versus it's worksheet." Additionally, you can go to the library or a bookstore to look at prep books to supplement the ones you already own. Look for books specifically geared toward the sections (English, Math, Verbal, Science...) you are working on—these books will often organize practice problems by topic, making it easy to find relevant problems. Like your prep book, the other prep books will have problems modeled after those used in the official tests. You can even go through tests you've previously completed and look for similar problems.

Keep practicing until you are comfortable. When you feel like you've mastered a few new techniques, do another practice section to gather more data. In this way, we've established a cycle: do a section, gather information about the skills you need to practice, practice those skills, do a new section, gather new information. The next time you do a practice section, you will also see if you were able to apply the skills you practiced based on the results of your previous test.

Teaching

Often when people say, "Those who can't do, teach," they don't mean it in a positive way. But in test prep, the desire to build familiarity with material is a great reason to teach. Nothing will make you step up to the plate like having to teach information to someone else. I'm using the term *teach* loosely. The element of teaching that matters here is talking through information out loud, whether there is an audience or not. In your test prep, it is useful to teach anything, from a general concept to a problem set.

Before giving an explanation, you need to do the necessary prep work to understand the principles behind the concept or problem under discussion. This prep work could consist of already having completed a problem set or having reviewed an idea to the point that you are ready to attempt explaining it. As you teach someone (or the stuffed animal that, if anyone asks, has been in storage since you were twelve), you will observe where you stumble—and that's a cue that you need to go back and study some more. If you are teaching a person, he or she can also ask questions, engaging you in a dialogue that forces you to become clearer in your logic and understanding of the concept and its application within the problem. If your initial explanation confuses your student, you will be challenged to devise an alternative way of explaining it.

Focus on Specific Objectives

Beyond having goals that will be realized in the future, it is equally important to have a clear intention every time you sit down to work with the test. When you sit down to do your test prep, take a moment to reflect on what you want to accomplish before you begin your work. Setting an objective for a given prep session will propel you to take the steps to achieve that end.

The power of intention lies not in empty words, but in the sentiment behind the words and the actions that logically follow. Consider the qualitative difference between a general statement like, "I want to do a Math section," and a specific statement like, "I want to do math drills to improve my pacing" or "I want to do a Math section so that I feel proud of the work that I did today. I want to feel a sense of accomplishment. Even if in today's session I am not able to achieve the results that I ultimately want on the test, I want to know that I took purposeful actions toward achieving those results."

Which student do you think is more likely to set aside the time to do his or her work? Which student do you think is more likely to focus during his or her practice session?

As we proceed, consider your intentions around the smaller steps of test prep, and become clear about what specifically you can do to support your intentions.

Practice Doesn't Make Perfect

"Practice doesn't make perfect. Perfect practice makes perfect." This turn of phrase, often credited to football coach Vince Lombardi, sheds a new light on an old cliché, and it's worth applying to your test prep. It isn't enough to do problems; you should do them to the best of your ability and review the mistakes you've made when you're done with every section. The goal isn't literal perfection, of course. Rather, the goal is to work with as much focus, determination, efficiency, and proficiency as possible.

Perfect practice means not only approaching your test preparation with the right mindset, but also giving yourself the right testing environment. Minimize avoidable distractions. You will never take the official ACT or SAT with a television blaring in the background, so don't practice under such conditions. Avoidable distractions needn't be as egregious as a television; sometimes they come as a temptation to play music, a visit from your family pet, or a cell phone alert. Close the door, and leave your phone in the other room or switch it to airplane mode to avoid being interrupted by notification pings.

Once an ACT student came to me panicked because she went over time when taking a Math section while on a bus from New York to DC. Well, of course she went over time! The bus was jostling her up and down and she was surrounded by other people who were going about their own bus ride business. A few days later she finished a similar section under the time limit and scored in the 30s.

For perfect practice, you must be focused and purposeful. Work in a quiet environment, free of distractions. Complete entire sections in their full allotted time—don't stop midway through to get a snack or do something else. If you are doing a drill, keep clear, specific records of your goal, the stipulations of the drill, and how you performed within the limitations you set for yourself—I'll give you more detailed suggestions for record keeping in the next chapter. When practicing for your standardized test, you should be in it to win it, and your mindset and environment should support that objective, because setting yourself up for success improves the likelihood of succeeding.

The Real World: Dealing with Less-Than-Ideal Conditions

You are feeling good. You know what it takes to accurately measure your test prep progress and create perfect practice. But then, it happens: suboptimal practice conditions. You didn't sleep enough last night (or the last five nights). You are working in the noisy cafeteria. You have twenty minutes to do a twenty-five-minute section. What to do? Should you skip the prep altogether, holding out for a day when you can bring your A-game?

Probably not.

Sure, ideal testing conditions are…ideal. We want them on test day, and we want them during preparation. However, it would be foolish to wait for well-rested alertness, lack of homework, solitude, and a prime daily horoscope to coincide. Create the best circumstances for your test prep that you can, but don't compromise your test prep altogether if the circumstances are less than ideal.

Circumstances aren't an excuse to give 50 (or 0) percent effort. Think of obstacles as a part of the challenge. While I don't endorse designing all of your prep sessions around extraneous obstacles— isn't the test challenge enough?—if you find yourself in a noisy cafe, overtired, or with less time than you want, do the prep work to the best of your ability. The constraints can strengthen your mettle and serve to mimic the more stressful conditions of test day.

Think of my student riding the bus. She felt discouraged by her performance, yet it was merely a reflection of the less-than-ideal circumstances. Sure, if she could ace the test on a bus, she could probably ace it anywhere; but not acing the test on a bus was hardly an indication that she couldn't score well elsewhere. Adjust your expectations, and don't be too hard on yourself if you identify a factor in your practice session that hampered your performance. Use the information as constructive feedback. If your score drops when you sleep for four hours the night prior to a practice section, it shows that you need more than four hours of sleep in order to focus and perform up to your standards.

There's much that you can control in your prep sessions and your test-day experience, but there will also be elements beyond your control, including distractions. You never know if the person next to you will have the sniffles. Or the hiccups. Or a nervous habit of pencil tapping. Heck, one of my New York City students took a test while protesters demonstrated beneath the test-room windows.

The worst distractions I dealt with during my college admissions test process came during an official ACT when the high school's marching band drum line was practicing on the football field directly adjacent to the test room. Even now, as I recall that morning, I can hear the metronome beating. Needless to say, this was highly distracting and upsetting. I informed the fine people at ACT about what had happened, and they graciously included a note about the incident with that day's score report.

Your bedroom or a study is certainly good for practically perfect test prep, but to expect such privacy and stillness elsewhere—including the test center—is unrealistic. While you may never have a drum line rehearsal or a full-on protest occurring outside the test room, there's a good chance that there will be distractions. To prepare yourself, you ought to occasionally practice outside of your home.

Public libraries are great for practice tests. They are quiet, but not silent. There are more distractions than you would normally find in a formal test setting, but fewer than you would find in a coffee shop.

It's good to know how you perform as your best self under ideal quiet, controlled circumstances. But it can be informative and incredibly helpful to branch out, too.

CHAPTER 7
AFTER TIME IS UP

The buzzer on your phone may signal that the official time is up, but it needn't cut off your potential to learn from the practice test. *Au contraire*. After time is up is when the real test prep magic begins! Utilizing this window will sharpen your skills like nothing else.

I'll start this chapter by telling you the step that hardly anyone knows to take—even though it's a terrific way to boost your technique. While I'm at it, I'll give you a few little-known insights into correcting your practice tests.

Then, we'll talk about the mindset of correcting practice tests and the way you should end every practice session.

Post-Test Review

Respecting time limits while taking a test or doing a practice section helps you to build effective time management skills for test day. On the other hand, it may not leave you much (or any) time to check your work or solve challenging problems. These are important skills, too—skills that will improve your test-taking abilities and, ultimately, your score—and you don't need to compromise them simply because you aren't yet finishing with time to spare.

Once you've finished a timed section, before scoring your test, go back through the test. Spend as much time as you wish solving the problems that required additional effort and trying to catch any wrong answers before you score the timed practice. Use a separate sheet of paper to record your new answers so that your bubble sheet provides a record of how you scored within the allotted time. Doing the extra work in an untimed setting gives you practice with problem solving, an opportunity to learn new techniques, and a chance to check your work with absolutely no external pressure.

If you are taking a full practice test, defer any additional review of individual sections until after you've gone through the whole test so as not to disrupt the flow of the test. Don't worry—you can take a break before doing your post-test review.

How to Correct Your Practice Test

Correcting your test might sound intuitive, but it isn't. In fact, it might be the most underestimated and underutilized aspect of the test prep process for overall performance improvement.

In your classes, when a test is returned to you, you are probably told which questions you answered incorrectly and given the correct answers immediately. Your first impulse when correcting a practice test likely mirrors this pattern. You think that, upon finishing a test, you should go to the back of the prep book, see which questions you answered incorrectly, read the correct answers and their explanations, and be done. But that isn't the most helpful approach to correcting your test for learning purposes. The more energy you invest in checking your test and understanding the questions you weren't fully confident in answering, the more you will improve at answering test questions.

Here are two far more useful techniques for correcting your test. You can choose one or the other, or start with the first option and supplement with the second.

1. Check your bubble sheet using the answer key. When you identify a question you answered incorrectly, put a tick mark at the top of your bubble sheet or on scrap paper, *not* next to the question you answered incorrectly. After checking all of the answers in a section, count how many questions you answered incorrectly. Then, go through the section and review your work, trying to identify the questions you answered incorrectly and come up with correct answers. Record your revised answers on a separate sheet of paper. Then, check your new answers. How many of the incorrect answers did you identify? How many incorrect answers did you successfully correct? Did you switch any correct answers to incorrect answers? This is excellent practice for both problem solving and checking your work during the timed test.

2. Check your bubble sheet using the answer key. Put an "X" next to any questions you answered incorrectly, but don't mark the correct answer. Then, go back to the questions you answered incorrectly, try to figure out where you went wrong, and select a different answer choice. If you narrowed down the answers to two or three options, now's your chance to select one of the answers you didn't choose previously.

Each of these methods involves checking your answers against the answer key, but they also involve follow-up work. Ideally, ask a friend or family member to check your answers for you so that you don't have to worry about accidentally remembering the incorrect questions or correct answers. If no one is available, you can check the answers yourself.

Once you've finished the blind corrections ("blind" meaning that you don't know the correct answers when reviewing the problems), you can review your answers using the answer key and explanations. The important question to ask when reviewing the problems you answered incorrectly is, "Why is the correct answer better than the one I chose?" Then, take the time to absorb the lessons that come from examining each wrong answer.

After reviewing the questions you answered incorrectly, it's time to consider the questions to which you guessed the correct answers, even if you answered them correctly. In each case, ask yourself, "Why is the correct answer better than the options I didn't eliminate?"

Other questions to consider when reviewing your work include:

- Did you underline within the problem?
- Did you show your work as you solved? (when applicable)
- Did you mark the answer choice you intended to mark based on the answer you found?
- Did you check your work after you finished your first pass through the test?

If you didn't do all of these, then you need to refine your test-taking technique. If you did all of these, then review the concept to which the problem relates.

Examine your wrong answers. By "examine" I don't mean "see what the right answer is" but closely evaluate your errors: determine where you went wrong, how you went wrong, and why you went wrong. Take time with your wrong answers. When you do this, you teach yourself how to avoid similar mistakes in the future. Plus, skills or problem styles that have challenged you in the past actually become confidence boosters. Every time you see them, they are reminders of how far you've come.

In a day or two, return to any problems you answered incorrectly and try to solve them. This also goes for questions to which you guessed the correct answer.

Learn from Your Mistakes

I get excited when my students answer questions incorrectly on practice sections. "You answered so many questions wrong! That's so great!" My reaction confuses them until I explain my enthusiasm.

Correcting and reviewing a practice test is a means of collecting data. Whether a specific question was answered correctly or incorrectly is neither good nor bad—it is objective information that we will use to focus the direction of our work. In the Math section, if a student answers an averages problem incorrectly, guess what we have to study? Averages! Data is essential to targeted growth, just as it would be to a small start-up or a Fortune 500 company.

In preparing for the test, it's your job to find the weak links in your knowledge and technique so that you can fix them sooner rather than later. When you identify weaknesses in a practice section, you have time to address them so that you are better informed when taking the official test.

Ryan was a student who hated reviewing wrong answers. He didn't merely dislike going over wrong answers—he *hated* it. After finishing and scoring a section, he immediately wanted to move on to another one. He hoped that his mistakes would work themselves out with time. But without understanding your mistakes, there is no opportunity for improvement. All you will do is continue to make the same errors test after test. After all, if you don't know where you're going wrong, how could you possibly know how to go right? I compelled Ryan to look bravely and squarely at his mistakes. He tried to negotiate his way out of it, but I stood firm. If he wanted to make progress (and he did), ignoring his mistakes was not an option. After

Ryan started reviewing his mistakes the way I describe here, his SAT score went up 450 points in four weeks. Not too shabby.

Like Ryan, you might resist reviewing wrong answers. Incorrect answers might make you feel uncomfortable, vulnerable, frustrated, or even stupid. Remember, incorrect answers aren't bad; they are simply information that will help you do better next time, especially if you maximize their usefulness through examining your mistakes and learning from them.

The other day, when I was going over another student's test with her, she had this to say on making mistakes:

"If you aren't making mistakes, you probably aren't making anything at all."

So smart.

Luck and Magic

Luck is when you have some idea how to do something, take a chance, and hope for the best. Sometimes you win, sometimes you lose. Magic is what happens when you understand techniques so well that positive results follow naturally. Magic has a much higher success rate and is far more impressive.

In yoga, luck is kicking up into a headstand and hanging out upside down for two seconds. Magic is knowing how to position your body so that you can consistently and easily bring yourself up into the headstand and hold the position.

In tests, the difference between luck and magic is the difference between "happening into" a correct answer through guessing (educated or random) and achieving a correct answer through skill and knowledge. It is the difference between saying an answer "sounds right" and explaining why an answer choice is the only logical option.

Guessing is a part of skillful test taking. When checking your work after a practice test, you will likely see that some of your guesses were correct. There is gratification in finding out you guessed correctly, but it isn't good enough for the long haul. The fact that you guessed indicates that you haven't yet mastered the material covered in the question. After you have scored each practice test, be sure to review the questions you didn't answer with confidence, regardless of whether you answered them correctly. That way, when that topic is tested on future exams, you won't have to rely on luck.

The other cool thing about magic? Even if you know exactly how to achieve the desired ends, it doesn't take away from the thrill of achieving them.

Themes and Concepts

It's easy to think that the mistakes or missteps you discover while reviewing a test are rooted in the specific problems. You understand probability—you just misunderstood that question… Right?

Maybe. But if you answered a probability question incorrectly or guessed its answer, it's worth reviewing the general themes and concepts related to the test question. When you are reviewing a test, continue to ask yourself, "What concept is being tested here?" Once you've identified the concept, study it. By reviewing the underlying concepts, you will begin to recognize them when they appear in different ways in different questions.

Try to notice patterns in your wrong answers. While there is power in looking at problems individually, there is greater power in identifying a trend that thematically connects multiple questions that you have answered incorrectly. For example, do you tend to flub grammar questions testing subject-verb agreement? Do you forget about little commas tacked onto the end of answer choices?

Similarly, if you bring a question to someone else for guidance, ask for an explanation of the underlying concepts, not just the problem itself.

"I know I ___"

Self-awareness is widely regarded as a positive attribute. When employed for your benefit, self-awareness is not an excuse for why things happened a certain way in the past or a preemptive excuse for future errors. Self-awareness spurs growth when you say, "I know I do that, so I'm going to look out for that kind of problem moving forward and take a specific action step so that I don't keep falling into the same trap." You could be confusing the uses of a comma and semicolon, forgetting to look at the labels of a graph's axes, mixing up like-sounding words, or forgetting to distribute a negative sign. Bringing awareness to whatever counterproductive pattern you've observed is the first step in changing it.

Self-awareness is a tool. Like all tools, it only works if you know how to use it. Self-awareness puts you in a rut when you say, "I know I do that," and move on. It can lull you into complacency when you accept the observation as "just the way it is" and, for that matter, the way it will always be. But so long as you remember that how you perform is dynamic, self-awareness is one of the best tools to help you get where you want to go.

Take Note

At the end of every prep session, take note of what you did during your session in your notebook. Doing so will help you reinforce what you have accomplished and clarify your future goals. Here are some topics you can address in your notes:

What You Did

- Date and time of the session
- What did you do to center yourself at the beginning of your session? (I'll suggest some centering activities in Chapter 9)

- How did you feel when you started? (rested/tired, focused/ distracted, calm/overwhelmed…)

- Which sections did you practice?

- How did you structure each section? (a drill, a complete section, a full practice test)

- What were your scores? (raw and scaled, when applicable)

- Where were you? What was the environment like?

Time

- Did you check your watch regularly to keep track of time?

- Were there specific questions you should have guessed at in the interest of improving efficiency?

If you worked within regulation time and finished your first pass within the time limits:

- How much time had elapsed when you finished your first pass?

If you worked within regulation time and didn't finish your first pass within the time limits:

- How many questions did you answer within the time limits?

- How many of the questions you didn't reach within the time limits did you answer correctly during your post-test review?

If you worked without time limits:

- How much time had elapsed when you finished your first pass?

- How much time had elapsed when you finished checking your work?

CHAPTER 8

MINDSET

All right, we've covered a lot of important practical tips for successful test prep. Along the way, we've also touched on elements of perspective and intentionality. Now, we're going to deepen our exploration of mindset as it relates to the ups and downs of test prep.

As you read, keep in mind these words from Martin de Maat: "You are pure potential."

Hit Me with Your Best Shot

People often throw around the phrase "do your best." But what does that mean?

Doing your best is an inside game. It is fueled by intention, and measured according to the actions that follow the intention. It's important that you strive to set yourself up with conditions—physical and mental—conducive to working optimally. Hold yourself accountable. You have people rooting for you, but ultimately you are doing this for yourself and your goals.

A person's "best" is not constant; it is dynamic. What constitutes your best on one day is not equal to what constitutes your best on another day. A recreational runner's best for a given day won't necessarily be a seven-minute mile, even if her body has the physical capability to run at that pace. Some days she will be in top form. Perhaps she will surpass her expectations and clock in under seven minutes. Other days, her best might be a ten-minute mile. Still others, she will need to walk it.

Off days will happen. In-the-zone days will happen. They happen to all of us—that's what makes us human, not robots. If you can walk away from an off day (or a great day!) knowing that you did your best, then let that be enough. Accept the results, and resume your efforts the next day.

Tennis

For a few years I trained at a highly respected acting studio in New York City. My acting teacher told us stories as a way to communicate ideas about acting and, as it turns out, life. While many of the stories are memorable, one about the learning process seems particularly apt for our purposes.

Let us imagine an acquaintance who has played tennis recreationally for a couple of years. He never trained in the sport; he just picked up a racket one day and started hitting a ball around. He continued to play, encouraged by his enjoyment of the game. Over time, he became pretty good. In fact, he won seven out of ten games against his friends.

All of that success had him thinking, "Wow. If I'm winning seven out of ten games now, imagine how good I could be if I took lessons!"

So, this person set up a lesson with a tennis instructor recommended by a friend who consistently gave him a run for his money on the tennis court.

"You're holding the racket wrong," the tennis instructor observed shortly into the first meeting, and proceeded to correct our friend's grip.

Isn't that great? Immediately, this guy is receiving feedback that will help his game improve so that he will start winning more games. Except the advice is followed by a strange turn of events: our friend starts losing.

Why would that be? Easy: he was in the habit of holding his racket the wrong way. Eventually, this new grip will serve him far better than the grip he was accustomed to; he will ultimately have a more powerful shot and better control. But for the time being, the grip is new, unfamiliar, and slightly uncomfortable. Every shot feels different when he holds the racket this new way.

So, what's our friend to do? Have patience and keep practicing. Pretty soon, he'll reap the rewards of improving his technique.

That's the way learning is. Sometimes, you have to get worse before you get better.

Progress Is Not Linear

You know the equation for a linear regression, right? $y = mx + b$. As x changes, y changes relative to x. It's predictable, straightforward, and functional.

The learning process is not linear. Progress is rarely steady. It is often filled with plateaus and, as the tennis story illustrates, setbacks. You reach a point when you think you're strong enough to add another element to your test-taking technique—sitting for longer sessions, stricter pacing within a section, showing your work more clearly on the page—but when you change things up, your score suffers or your pace slows. You panic. It wasn't supposed to happen like that. Maybe you were better off before, or maybe you're doomed to never achieve the satisfying results you've been working toward.

Never fear. This is part of the process. Stick with it and see if you improve.

Of course, if a plateau or setback lasts for an extended time, and you've been working consistently toward positive change, you might reassess and see if there is another tweak you could make to your technique to achieve results. For example, you might give yourself more time to check your work by moving more quickly through the first pass, or slow down your initial pace so that there are fewer errors at the outset. Or, go back to the "Teaching" or "Thinking Out Loud" learning techniques: talk through problems out loud to see where you are getting stuck. If you think your plateau might represent a peak, continue working with curiosity and enthusiasm. If you work consistently, your score might still improve from the skillful practice, or, if nothing else, you will maintain your skills.

The Bell Curve

If you haven't already discovered it when looking at score reports, let me introduce you to the standard bell curve.

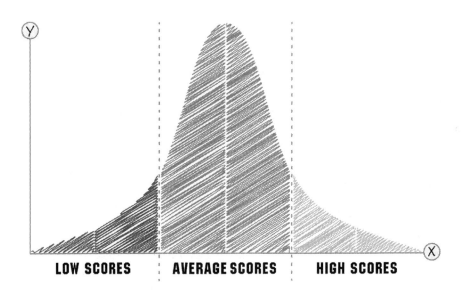

| LOW SCORES | AVERAGE SCORES | HIGH SCORES |

The bell curve is a crucial concept in statistics class. It illustrates the range in performance across a large sample. In the context of standardized tests, the bell curve shows the spread of test scores. Fewer people will score at either extreme—really, really good, or really, really bad—than in the mid-range. In the same way, every person has a bell curve that describes his or her range of possible scores if he or she took the test many, many times. The range of possibilities is much narrower for an individual than for a group, but it varies from test to test following the same pattern.

The bell curve applies to other contexts, as well. To return to our runner example, she might finish a mile in anywhere from seven minutes to ten minutes. The occasions when she completes a seven-minute mile are just as rare as when she finishes a ten-minute mile. Far more often, she will finish a mile in eight to nine minutes. Most often, she finishes in eight minutes, thirty seconds.

Part of the objective of training is to minimize the spread of your bell curve. Think of our friend, the recreational tennis player. There is likely a fair amount of variability in his performance from one day to the next. On the other hand, Serena and Venus Williams play far more consistently. If we were to rate their tennis performances on a scale of 1 to 100, their performances would not only have significantly higher average ratings than that of our friend, but there would also be less variation among their ratings from one game to the next.

As you continue to prep, your score should become more consistent, and external factors such as nerves will have less impact on your performance.

You Didn't Lose Everything You've Learned

Off days happen. When they happen, the most important thing to remind yourself is that you haven't forgotten everything you've learned. A drop in your score can be disheartening. But take a step back and look at the bigger picture.

If you have been working steadily and have had consistently higher scores, the odds are pretty low that some magnet wiped your brain clean and that you have to go back and relearn everything that you've spent months studying. More likely, something else was going on: you were working somewhere noisy, you were distracted, or maybe you were overtired. Any one of these would explain a drop in score and suggest modifications of your habits: sleep more, work from home or in a library, perform one of the "Keeping Clear" techniques introduced in the next chapter before you begin, and so on. Review the skills you need to review. But first and foremost, forgive yourself. The more compassionately you treat yourself, the easier it will be to objectively review what happened and trust that your test taking will go better in the future. Because I promise you, you didn't lose everything you've learned.

When Change Can't Happen Soon Enough

You began prepping for your test with more than fifteen years of life experience being you. That comes with certain habits—some good and some in need of refining. As you tackle the challenge of test prep, you will need to form new habits. Maybe your habits relate to test-taking technique, to a technical skill such as reading for detail, or to some content topics you need to refresh and refine. Maybe the habits relate to your self-talk or the way you connect to your goals. If you have habits that need reworking, you've probably been living with them longer than you've been prepping for the SAT or ACT. Give yourself a break. It takes time to establish new habits. The fact that you are open to acknowledging your weaknesses and to improving your technique means that you are already on the road to improvement.

You may not see results in your scores, but that doesn't mean you aren't improving. You could still be uncovering concepts that you need to review—perhaps you correctly answer a question about the topic you reviewed last week, but incorrectly answer a question about a concept that you've yet to review in depth. Or, it could simply be that your growth is happening in a subtle way that hasn't yet translated to your score. Remember, the learning process isn't linear. Sometimes your score will go up, sometimes it will go down, and sometimes it will plateau for a while. With consistent efforts and a broad perspective, you will see positive trends. A short-term plateau doesn't necessarily signify a peak unless you decide to stop where you are.

Believe that you will achieve your goal, and act accordingly. When you behave as someone who might achieve that goal would behave, you improve your chances of achieving the goal. Once you are doing everything in your power, you can begin trusting that the results that will come long-term.

When Everything's Going Great

I'm so glad that you are starting to see positive results from your test prep process. That should feel gratifying: all of your hard work—and I'm sure you've put in hard work if you are seeing results—is paying off! Take a moment to soak up how good it feels. It's worth enjoying the wins when they come.

Good, now that you've done that, a warning: don't slip into complacency. Once you've earned your goal score in a section for the first time, there's a temptation to slack off. "I know I had scheduled an hour to work on test prep today," you tell yourself, "but I'm doing all right, so it really couldn't hurt to skip today, could it?"

Yes. Yes, it could.

Mind you, I'm all for living a balanced life—we've discussed this. Fun, creative, or active diversions energize you so that when you return your focus to your work, you are more effective than you would have been otherwise. I'm all for breaks, and I'm all for giving yourself a little breather from the test prep process, which can sometimes grow quite intense.

However, don't mistake one or two high scores with having already beaten the test. If you didn't earn the score on the official test day, you haven't finished preparing.

Think of a pro basketball player. He doesn't stop practicing once he's made it to the NBA—he works harder. Like a muscle, your test-taking skills require conditioning. If you stop going to the gym, you will lose your six-pack abs. If you stop reviewing vocabulary, you will forget words. If you stop taking practice tests, you will lose your rhythm. That's the way it is.

Don't confuse the high that comes from a few good scores with the confidence that comes from consistently good scores. A couple of good scores does not a trend make. You aren't interested in individual scores; you care about trends. You want to work toward consistency. Once you consistently achieve the scores that you want, you will gain confidence, which is a natural response to feeling effective in a given area. Even if having reached your high score during practice doesn't count on test day, the confidence that comes from it does.

Also, consider whether you reached your goal score on a practice section or a full practice test. If you achieved your target score on a practice section, that means you are starting to handle the skills and techniques needed for that section. But it also means that when you took the section, you hadn't already done three other sections nor were you conserving energy for the three to nine sections still to come. Your energy and fatigue levels were different than they would be if you were completing a four-hour test. This does not devalue the achievement of scoring well in a section taken on its own, but scoring well in practice sections is a cue that you should start transitioning into full practice tests, not stop practicing altogether.

Stick with your prep schedule. When the great score report comes from ACT or the College Board, it will be worth it.

CHAPTER 9
KEEPING CLEAR

As you progress in your prep work, it's likely that you will encounter some resistance. Resistance may take the form of fear, anxiety, attention issues, apathy... Basically, resistance is anything that causes you to feel like less than your best self, thereby slowing your momentum.

Thankfully, there are tools that will help you to keep a clear, open, positive perspective in this process and in life. In this chapter, I will walk you through a few of my favorite tools. I've used all of these to deal with my own internal resistance.

Don't leave these in your toolbox. Use them regularly. Then, when you realize you need them, it will be second nature to pull them out, and they'll be more effective because you've practiced using them under less intense circumstances.

These right actions will consistently leave you feeling a little (or a lot) better than you felt before you did them.

Make Your Playlist Work for You

So you thought that your music collection worked best when you hit shuffle? Only came in handy while driving somewhere, at a party, or going for a run? Nope. Sure, music is fun and helpful in all of these scenarios. But we can up its value by transforming music from something that happens in the background of your experience to something that shapes your experience. You own music, and we can make that music work for you. Yes, there is a connection between your playlist and your test prep.

We've all heard that listening to Mozart increases your intelligence; that's not what I'm talking about. If you want to experiment with Mozart and see what happens, more power to you. But I'm not suggesting some passive panacea that will magically make you smarter. I'm talking about a practical tool that actually has the ability to affect the way you feel.

Music carries energy. I don't mean this in a woo-woo everything-is-energy kind of way. Music's energy is observable. Think about the music you listen to. Different songs affect you in different ways. Songs can make you feel optimistic, energized, angry, hurt, powerful, contemplative, silly, defiant, sad, joyful, hopeful, or proud. When you are in a good mood, you don't want to listen to that depressing song about a break-up, so you skip past it. When you aren't cast in the role you want in the school play, you might prefer an angry punk song over a song extolling how awesome everything is. Generally, people try to find music that matches how they already feel. Usually that's fine, but sometimes a person's emotional state stands in his or her way. Beyond finding music that matches how you already feel, you can also use music to shift your mood into the one that you want to feel. You might already do this in certain circumstances without even realizing it. You probably have certain songs that you play while working out, spending time with friends, or getting ready for the day. These songs create a certain mood that enhances your experience. You can apply this mechanism to finding songs that set the tone for your test prep.

How do you want to feel while taking your SAT or ACT? You want to feel smart, I'm sure, but there may not be many songs in your collection that make you feel smart (well, maybe the Mozart). Be that as it may, there are songs that make you feel empowered. Calm. Centered. Energized. Strong. Carefree. Optimistic.

One of my clearest memories from high school is a morning when I was driving to an AP test. It felt like an entire year's worth of work—plus the more recent period of intense review—was coming to a head. As I was driving, "The Remedy" by Jason Mraz came on my car audio system. There's a line in the chorus in which Mraz declares freedom from the worries that have bogged him down. It was exactly what I needed to hear. By the time I arrived at the parking lot, I felt freer and in a better state to focus on the test. I was ready to go.

Decide how you want to feel, then make a playlist of the songs in your music library that elicit this feeling. The playlist can be as long or as short as you wish. Maybe you choose two or three songs that create your desired mood every time you hear them. Maybe you include thirty songs because you prefer variety.

Listen to your playlist before your prep sessions. You don't need to listen to the whole playlist every time you sit down. Listen until you feel focused, confident, and ready. You can also go back to using shuffle on your curated playlist. Because you've designed your playlist with the intention of rocking the test (pun intended), any and all of the songs you've chosen will mentally prepare you for the task at hand.

Write It Out

One of my favorite warm-ups for test taking involves a few blank sheets of paper and a pencil. Before a test or practice session, put your pencil to paper and write. It's that simple.

You write. And you write. And you write.

You keep writing for about three lined pages or twelve-ish minutes.

Whatever thought comes up, you write down. No one will read what you write—possibly not even you. You don't need to write in complete sentences. You don't need to stay on topic. You don't need to write anything profound. You just write, stream-of-consciousness style. This exercise externalizes the thoughts that are cluttering up your internal process, leaving you clear, calm, and focused.

Hannah, the first student to whom I suggested stream-of-consciousness writing, was someone who experienced attention difficulties. She didn't have extended time testing accommodations, but she did have trouble focusing. By writing down her thoughts—thoughts that would remain in her head, distracting her, if she didn't write them down—Hannah was able to clear her mind and focus on the test.

Stream-of-consciousness writing functions like the Pensieve that Dumbledore uses in *Harry Potter*. Dumbledore takes a silvery thread of thought and drops it into the Pensieve. All of the thoughts Dumbledore removes exist after he extracts them. But through his use of the Pensieve, Dumbledore is able to externalize them so that they don't interfere with his clarity in the present moment. Similarly, when you write down thoughts to clear your mind, all of the thoughts are safe on paper. You can deal with them after the test, if you want to, but they won't bother you during the test.

The thoughts that you write down have nothing to do with the actual test. Even if they relate to the idea of the test, they don't specifically relate to the problems in front of you. How could they? You haven't seen the test yet!

As time passed, I continued to give this exercise to other students, and I had a cool realization: it's a one-size-fits-all centering exercise and performance booster. It can be used by a student with attention issues or test anxiety or anyone who wants to prepare mentally for the test. This exercise creates a new mental space in which to operate. If you think of any activity in which you participate —theater, music, dance, sports, etc.—before you "perform" you have a warm-up or centering exercise to separate what you were focusing on in the "real world" (school, homework, friends, driving, television, music, siblings) from the space that you are about to perform in, both physical (the stage, the court, the field) and mental (focused, clear, energized, ready).

Stream-of-consciousness writing has neither rubric nor rules. Your only guide is to transcribe your thoughts without judgment, critique, or pause. Maybe your pre-test writing will look like this:

Here I am getting ready to take another ACT. I don't know why Erika recommended that I do this pre-writing thing. I mean, I know she explained it to me, but it just feels like a waste of time. Don't I have enough to do with four hours of testing ahead of me? Ugh four hours. Four hours is so long. I don't want to be here for four hours. On one hand it's like, "Is it test day yet?" but on the other it's like "No, never come test day! Never come!" I'm just so nervous. Ugggh. I really want to get into a good school and if I don't it will suck and what if I do badly on this test? I mean, I know this is just a practice test but come on it's still serious you know?

Or maybe it will look like this:

My mom made me angry today. I wanted to go to the concert next weekend and she said no and it makes me mad because I really want to go to the concert and my friends are going and it is unfair and I don't want to do my prep which has nothing to do with the concert but still. Anyways. So test prep. I better snap out of it. I have to get ready for this test. I can't go to the concert but I am going to kick ass on the SAT. I've been feeling really good about things lately. I've been studying vocab and learning lots of new words. Yesterday I used one and Joey was like, "Dude that's a big word." And I felt pretty good. Articulate. Words are cool. Ha.

Or, maybe (on a good day) it will look like this:

I'm so psyched! I'm doing so well in school and I've been doing really well on my test prep and yesterday I got my highest score yet and all of this is really working and I am awesome and life is cool and I wore my new shoes today and I'm reading this really great book. I normally get distracted when I'm reading but this book is so good I can hardly put it down and there was this really interesting article on the NYT website today. I want to move to New York!!! It is so cool there. I really hope I can visit for colleges. That would be so great. I love New York.

These stream-of-consciousness reflections are quite random. You would never submit any writing like this to a teacher. You probably don't write like this in a journal. It doesn't matter. The point is to write and follow your thoughts. Try it out. Anytime. You can try it now, if you want. I'll wait…

Okay, done? How did it go? Awesome! I'm glad you liked it! (Or, if you didn't, stick with it a few more times and see if it grows on you.)

Some students feel concerned that many of the thoughts they write down are negative. They worry that stream-of-consciousness writing puts them in a worse mood. However, you won't write down anything that isn't on your mind. It simply won't happen. If you're not worrying about the weather, it won't even occur to you to write about it. I don't want you to focus on finding negative thoughts, but if how you feel includes negative thoughts, write them down.

On the flip side, you might connect to a wise internal voice that knows exactly the right thing to say to you to improve your state of mind. Let's say that student number one from above kept writing (she's the one who was nervous about what a big deal the ACT is because she wants to get into a good school). What might happen next?

I mean I'm a generally really smart person. And I feel this pressure a lot, but honestly I think I am just way too hard on myself. I just need to relax. Really, it will all be okay. I mean, maybe it won't be, but I can't worry about that right now because I have a test to take. And honestly even though I haven't reached my goal score yet, I'm doing pretty well and I'm learning new things and applying them. I haven't gotten any Pythagorean theorem questions wrong since reviewing them the other day so that's awesome. I think I will be okay. I really do. I just need to stick with it and be consistent and it will all work out in the end. I know it will. I am ready. I am ready. I am ready. Let's do this.

By the end that student is in a much better mood. In fact, she's giving herself a little pep talk! She shifted her focus, and in so doing facilitated her ability to focus on the test instead of on her nerves. She opened herself up to the possibility of feeling better. Then, in came the more positive perspective and pep talk that she needed to emerge from her anxious funk. When you feel like you've released your extraneous thoughts, open yourself up to insights from the wise, calm, caring voice that exists beyond all the mental noise.

Your use of stream-of-consciousness writing can extend beyond the test. Maybe you will use it after you receive a bad grade and want to feel better in time for your next class, where you have an important presentation. Or maybe you are distracted by all of the things you have to do to the point that you can't focus on what your teachers are saying. Take out some notebook paper, start writing, and see what happens.

Hannah, the first student with whom I shared this technique, loved it so much that she started stream-of-consciousness writing not only before practice tests, but also before tests in school. Some students stream-of-consciousness write every morning before they leave for school—not in preparation for a test, but in preparation for life. Some students use it when they begin to feel emotionally overwhelmed. In each case, it's a game changer.

NOTE: According to official regulations, you may not bring scratch paper into either the SAT or the ACT testing rooms, but you can still write it out on test-day morning before signing in at the test center.

Meditation

I began meditating during my junior year of college. For several years, it fell into the category of "Things I Should Do" but that I didn't do regularly. Now that I meditate daily, it's like I've discovered a secret that I want everyone to know about, even though lots of other people know about it and the practice is thousands of years old.

Meditation is an effective way of clearing the stress that you accumulate throughout your day. With less stress weighing you down and distracting you, you can more effectively attend to life (which includes the SAT and ACT) when you aren't meditating. Meditating twice a day—once in the morning, and once in the early evening between lunch and dinner—also charges you up so that you can feel energized throughout your day, including the latter part of the day when your energy levels may be depleted. If you are willing to meditate for five minutes in the morning and five minutes after school, that's an excellent place to start. Or you can begin by meditating once a day for ten to fifteen minutes at a time that's convenient for you. Personally, I experience amazing benefits—including greater calm, increased energy, and improved focus—through meditating for twenty minutes in the morning and twenty minutes early in the evening.

During meditation you sit, eyes closed, and center yourself. Contrary to what some people believe, you don't need to stop thinking to meditate. That instruction would be sort of like the common challenge, "Don't think of a pink elephant." Once given the task, it's impossible to do anything but its opposite. Of course, it is nice when you reach a point in your meditation when you become aware of the space between your thoughts or the consciousness beyond your thoughts, but that isn't the goal per se. The goal is simply to sit and give yourself the period of stillness in which to release stress and recharge your energy. Meditation is process-oriented, not results-oriented.

In Vedic meditation, the form of meditation that I practice daily, thoughts are regarded as evidence of "unstressing." If you sit to meditate and thoughts arise, the thoughts indicate that you are releasing stress, and the meditation is working! At times it isn't particularly pleasant to experience the thoughts buzzing around in your mind—this is why many people claim, "I have too many thoughts to meditate"—but all of those thoughts are the reason to meditate. If you can sit with the thoughts for twenty minutes, you will experience hours of more peaceful, focused living during the rest of your day.

Here's a basic approach to meditation.

Close your eyes, and let yourself settle in for about thirty seconds. Allow your thoughts to unwind and your body to soften. Then, bring your attention to your breath.

Inhale…exhale…inhale…exhale… Take a moment to be grounded in your physical body. Feel the chair (or floor) beneath you and the sky above you; feel your back and feel your front. Become aware of the moment between the inhale and the exhale when your lungs are filled, ready to release, and the moment between the exhale and the inhale when your lungs are empty, ready to be filled. What does it feel like to breathe? What sensations do you notice?

As you meditate, you can repeat a word or short phrase with your inner voice or you can continue to observe your breath. This is when thoughts will arise. At first, you'll just be thinking. (This is the unstressing.) Then, you'll be aware that you are thinking. As soon as the awareness kicks in, bring your attention easily and effortlessly back to your original point of attention—the word, your breath… whatever you've chosen to focus on, return to it. Easily allow your attention to be with the word or your breath.

This pattern repeats. Thoughts arise. You become aware of the thoughts, and you bring your attention back. There is no score here. No grades. No good or bad, right or wrong. Your only responsibility is to sit down for the meditation. From there, the meditation will do exactly what it is supposed to do.

Another form of meditation involves visualization with your "inner eye" (the part of you that "sees" what you are dreaming or imagining even though your eyes are closed and you aren't actually flying or performing in the circus). I once suggested that a student meditate with the image of standing under a rain shower of SAT points. The idea of being gifted with an abundance of points enhanced her confidence and peace of mind, in turn helping her feel calm and clear while taking the test.

A wide selection of resources exists regarding different meditation techniques. The techniques offer different benefits and experiences. You can also find videos on YouTube and albums for purchase featuring guided meditations. Explore and have fun. Meanwhile, remember you don't need anything from the outside to meditate. No earplugs, no computer, no music player, no headphones. Your breath is always with you.

If you don't feel like researching meditation, start by sitting in a quiet place, closing your eyes, and bringing your attention to your breath, as referenced above. That's it. If you are doing that, then you are doing it right. Even if you begin to feel antsy, you are doing it right. Even if you open your eyes after thirty seconds, you are doing it right. Eventually you will be able to meditate for longer periods. And, no matter how many times you open your eyes to check the time, you always have the choice to close them again and return to your meditation.

Meditation has become an important tool in maintaining my well-being. I feel lucky to have discovered meditating when I did, and now I'm paying that gift forward to you. The benefits of regular meditation are widely recognized. If meditation appeals to you, I fully encourage you to try it. You don't have much to lose by experimenting.

The Fear Factor

One technique psychologists offer for dealing with fear is what I call the "And then what?" technique. For example, if you worry that you won't do well on your practice test, ask yourself the question, "What if I don't do well? Then what happens?"

Maybe your answer is, "I'll feel really bad."

Ask yourself again, *"And then what?"*

You reply, "I'll know how stupid I am."

"And then what?"

"I'll call up my friend Kate and complain about the test."

"And then what?"

"Maybe I'll watch TV to distract myself."

"And then what?"

"I'll stay up late doing my homework because I wasted so much time."

"And then what?"

"I won't get enough sleep and I'll be tired tomorrow."

"And then what?"

"I'll be cranky."

"And then what?"

"I'll probably take a nap at some point."

"And then what?"

"I'll feel a little better."

"And then what?"

"I'll probably go back to studying for my ACT."

Your "And then what?" exercise will likely lead you away from your negative experience of having done, by your estimation, poorly on your practice test. Time has a way of sweeping us up and carrying us through difficulties until the circumstances don't feel so bad or intense anymore. What you will come to realize is that events have only as much weight as you give them. Maybe in the moment a bad test score will feel like the end of the world and definitive proof that you are stupid, but it more likely indicates that you have a little more work to do. And as we talked about earlier, a low score provides specific guidance to identify the areas in which you need to do the work. By forcing yourself to ask what happens after your worst-case scenario, you will eventually see that your worst-case scenario isn't so bad after all. You can and will keep moving forward.

One caveat: when we are caught up in fear, it is easy to lose perspective. Instead of diffusing the situation, you create a succession of disappointments.

"I do poorly on the practice test."

"And then what?"

"I keep doing poorly on practice tests."

"And then what?"

"I do poorly on the real test."

"And then what?"

"I don't get into any college in America or the world."

"And then what?"

"I work at [insert worst-case-scenario job here] for the rest of my life."

"And then what?"

"I get sick and die."

As extreme as this sequence sounds, a bad score may feel like a tragedy. If you feel hopeless for a little while, accept it. Let the feeling be okay. But listen for a soft voice calmly reminding you that although things may feel hopeless right now, feeling that way doesn't make it true. Much more likely than total demise? You call your friend Kate, maybe stay up too late watching television or reading articles on the Internet, and are a little tired at school the next day. And then you get back to work.

Movement, Sleep, and Food for Thought

Your brain is part of your body. Sure, that seems self-evident enough, but it is easy to behave in a way that disregards this basic fact. We skip meals or eat junk food between meals. We drink beverages that aren't good for us. We sit around all day. We don't sleep enough. These habits take a toll on our bodies, but we let them slide in the name of convenience or because there are other things that seem more pressing than a wholesome meal or a full night's sleep. To a certain extent, our bodies are highly efficient machines that can compensate for the occasional overtaxing. You don't eat enough, sleep enough, move enough, or hydrate enough for one or two days? "No problem," your body says, "I will just work a little harder to make up for it."

But if you chronically don't eat, sleep, or move in a way that benefits your body, the strain will cause your body to function less efficiently. And, yes, your brain is a part of your body. If you want to do as well as possible on the test, you need to take care of your body. Eat well. Exercise. Sleep.

Often, when our eating habits don't serve us, we aren't aware of their deleterious effects because we've acclimated to feeling tired, hungry, sluggish, or uncomfortable. One way to see if your food choices work for you is to check in periodically throughout the day and track your energy levels. If you have a muffin for breakfast, how do you feel at ten o'clock? What about oatmeal? Eggs? Cereal? A banana? When planning meals, I've found food blogs to be helpful and inspiring.

Exercise is another important tool for your body—and, thus, your brain. It doesn't happen exclusively in gyms. It happens going for a walk, hike, or run. On a bike or a yoga mat. Shooting hoops in the driveway. Dancing to your favorite song. Getting down with an exercise video. The point is to move your body. Exercise helps release the negative energy that makes you feel overwhelmed and elevates the positive energy that helps you be effective and efficient. You enjoy post-exercise endorphins. You think clearly. Then, after all that exercise and productivity, you fall asleep easily at night and wake up without an alarm clock.

Which brings us to the importance of sleep. I don't know about you, but I sometimes feel a love-hate relationship with sleep. Sleep can feel like leaving the party. Sure, there will be another day, but what about all of the things I set out to achieve today? However, for the sake of those other days, it is important that I leave the party for a little while. It's not a luxury; it's a necessity. When I'm tired, all of my other coping mechanisms are compromised. High schoolers need to wake up early, so staying up late is burning the candle at both ends. Eventually, the fire goes out, and you're not left with much of value.

If you feel that there just isn't enough time for movement, good food, and sufficient sleep, examine your schedule and see if you can make your day more efficient so you can take thirty minutes to move your body or an extra hour to rest at night. There are plenty of instances when I sleep for fewer hours than I would like or make less-than-ideal food choices. But less than ideal is different from bad. I rarely make flat-out bad choices. This isn't because I'm so awesome at life; it's because I want to be so awesome at life. I do everything in my power to set myself up for success, and you can, too. A healthy lifestyle does not require being perfect. It requires building good habits.

Good feelings compound the more you practice good habits. Take actions that will help you make the most of yourself and receive the most from your life. Read books or articles on these topics, if it helps. Healthy habits will improve the quality of your day-to-day life mentally, emotionally, and physically. The healthier your body is, the better off your brain is. The better off your brain is, the clearer and more cogent your thinking. And the clearer your thinking, the better your test-taking skills.

Peer Chitchat

The halls of high schools are abuzz with chitchat on a wide variety of topics. There's gossip about relationships, activities, plans for the weekend...

Occasionally, the discussion may turn to test prep. When it does, it's likely that the conversation won't end with the bell. Rather, it will continue to echo in your mind:

"Madeline is doing the SAT, and she seems to really like it. Should I switch? Or maybe prep for both?"

"James has a tutor for the SATs. Kyle is taking a prep class. And I haven't worked with anyone. I'm screwed."

"Everyone says the test is always harder on test day. Should I be worried?"

Sometimes insights into another person's process will be helpful; other times they won't. Peer chitchat becomes a liability when it sends you into a tizzy of worries about doing the wrong thing, the different thing, or not enough of the right thing. Here's the real thing: everyone's journey is unique, and you can't define your path by that of someone else. Your goal is to figure out what is right for you. You decide which test to take, the best approach to a Reading section, which vocab list (or flash cards, or app) to use. Sometimes staying focused on your own journey will feel easier than other times. The more centered you are, the more connected you will be to the right approach for you and the less that peer chitchat will bother you.

You will be faced with the question of "Am I doing enough?" when so-and-so is doing this, that, and the other. You alone can answer this. Are you doing the best you can with the resources—time, teachers, prep books, library cards—available to you? If the answer is yes, then don't worry about what so-and-so is doing. Recommit to doing your best, and charge forward.

Insecurities can be alchemized into motivators. If you find out that someone else scored well, gained admission to a school you respect, or has a great prep regimen, there are two basic reactions: feel inspired or feel insecure. If you feel insecure, become aware of your reaction and ask yourself what your negative feelings are trying to tell you. Ask if there is something more you could be doing. If an answer comes, great—do that! If the answer is that you are taking the right actions in this moment, then stick with your plan and move forward confidently. Keep in mind that success isn't a zero-sum game. One person's success or happiness isn't dependent upon another's unhappiness. Sure, schools have limited slots, and tests are graded on a curve, but there are infinite opportunities for happiness and avenues toward success.

Adults

You have adults in your life. The kinds of relationships you have with them, and the extent of their involvement in your test prep process, vary greatly. That said, if you find your parents (for example) bothersome, you wouldn't be the first sixteen-year-old to feel that way, and you won't be the last. I can tell you that in most cases parents and other adults are doing their best, but they are also imperfect because they're human.

If you perceive your parents as grating, pressuring, disappointed, or anxious, my best advice is to forgive them. Forgiving most often happens when you are able to retreat to your own corner, take a deep breath, and decide that it isn't worth carrying the grievance. Forgiveness doesn't need to happen immediately, and it doesn't need to involve a conversation: *"I forgive you for asking me for the tenth time if I've done my prep."* I don't suggest forgiveness because I'm on their side, but because I'm on your side. Ultimately, this remains your process, your life. And the more negativity you carry—toward your parents or anyone else—the more weighed down and stressed out you will feel. I don't want you to feel burdened—I want you to feel empowered. Knowing that you can decide how you relate to any situation is empowering.

The other side of forgiveness is appreciation, and I'm guessing the adults in your life also do a lot right. Focus on this, too. Feel gratitude for the fact that they care about you and want you to succeed, and forgive them for the rest.

It's a moment-to-moment exercise, but the more you can let go of the frustration over how other people do or don't treat you, the more energy and focus you will have for the aspects of your life that are important to you...and your test prep. This is about you: your goals, ambitions, hopes, and dreams. Everything and everyone else is simply context. Take a breath, and bring your focus back to yourself.

Keep Showing Up

Prepare to meet resistance. It will come. There will be days when you don't feel like working on test prep. There will be days when you do feel like working on it, but you don't seem to be at your maximum performance level. Since you can expect days such as these, you can also prepare to persist despite the resistance. Identify the specific tools that help you out of your funk. Stream-of-consciousness write. Listen to music. Go for a walk. If you persevere through the days when you don't feel as purposeful or productive, another day will come when you feel better again. You will achieve positive results, but you must continue to show up along the way.

The most difficult days when starting a new routine, such as test prep, usually come after the initial surge of inspiration, but before you've done the routine long enough that it feels like a regular part of your life. It takes approximately forty days to form a habit. If you can make it through those early days of incorporating test prep into your schedule, not only will you likely see progress, but you will also have an easier time working test prep into your life in the weeks to come.

AN EASY-TO-FOLLOW FLOW CHART TO GUIDE YOUR TEST PREP

Okay, so you appreciate all of the advice, but you want direction that's a little more structured, a little more linear, a little less "trust your gut"?

Here you go.

Flip the page to see a flow chart that illustrates potential solutions for some of the issues that may come up during your test prep.

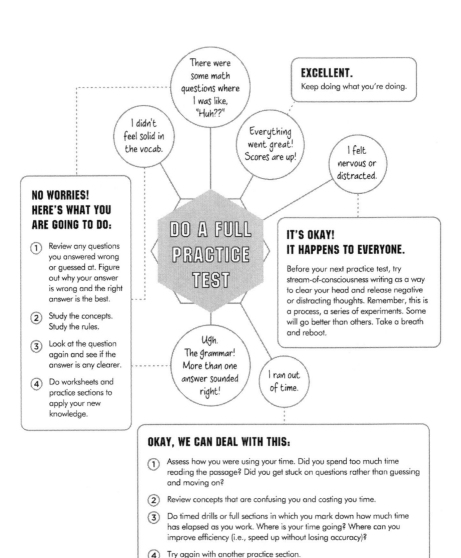

There were some math questions where I was like, "Huh??"

I didn't feel solid in the vocab.

Everything went great! Scores are up!

EXCELLENT.
Keep doing what you're doing.

I felt nervous or distracted.

DO A FULL PRACTICE TEST

NO WORRIES! HERE'S WHAT YOU ARE GOING TO DO:

(1) Review any questions you answered wrong or guessed at. Figure out why your answer is wrong and the right answer is the best.

(2) Study the concepts. Study the rules.

(3) Look at the question again and see if the answer is any clearer.

(4) Do worksheets and practice sections to apply your new knowledge.

IT'S OKAY! IT HAPPENS TO EVERYONE.

Before your next practice test, try stream-of-consciousness writing as a way to clear your head and release negative or distracting thoughts. Remember, this is a process, a series of experiments. Some will go better than others. Take a breath and reboot.

Ugh. The grammar! More than one answer sounded right!

I ran out of time.

OKAY, WE CAN DEAL WITH THIS:

(1) Assess how you were using your time. Did you spend too much time reading the passage? Did you get stuck on questions rather than guessing and moving on?

(2) Review concepts that are confusing you and costing you time.

(3) Do timed drills or full sections in which you mark down how much time has elapsed as you work. Where is your time going? Where can you improve efficiency (i.e., speed up without losing accuracy)?

(4) Try again with another practice section.

CHAPTER 10
LEADING UP TO TEST DAY

It's coming! Can you believe it?

In this chapter, we'll start by discussing a good attitude to have when you enter your first officially administered SAT or ACT. Then, I'll give you my best advice for approaching the week before the test right up to the night before. We'll also talk about some common concerns leading up to test day. This will help you feel grounded, purposeful, and on target.

Test Run

So long as you aren't taking the test for the first time in December of your senior year, a particular test date never needs to be the winning test date, and this is especially true the first time you take an officially administered test. The first time you take the SAT or ACT "for real," take it with the intention of experiencing the test rather than earning a specific score. Consider it a test run. No matter how many practice tests you take, nothing prepares you for taking the official test better than taking the official test.

Remember how I compared taking a full practice test on a Saturday morning to a play's dress rehearsal? Well, some productions also stage previews so that the cast can perform for a general audience, another element that changes the experience for the actors, before the press reviews a play on opening night. This is what it's like to take an officially administered test for the first time, if you have the option of taking the test more than once. Or, consider a sport's preseason. Playing in uniform against another team in front of fans feels different from scrimmaging in a closed practice. Scrimmaging in a closed practice feels different from running drills.

Previews and preseason games don't count toward an official record; they allow the participants to perform under circumstances that approximate those which they will need to deal with down the line.

Take for granted that the scores from the first time you take an officially administered test will not be the scores that college admissions officers ultimately use to evaluate your application. Sure, you will receive an official score report, but that doesn't need to determine your attitude about the first official test. You can still treat it like it's part of your test prep. Get your first test out of the way early in the process, and don't worry about what your score report will say. You might use your scores to direct your study plan. But remember that for the most part, your first time in the official test room is about the experience, not the score.

The Week before the Test

Given that you are accustomed to an academic study schedule, you probably think of the week before any test as the time to study. In the case of SAT/ACT test prep, come the week before the test, your studying is essentially complete—at least with regard to the upcoming Saturday test date. If you've been prepping consistently, you know everything you need to know, and there isn't much you could learn the week before the test that would make or break your scores. You're solid on the formulas, you have a huge arsenal of vocabulary words (not that learning an extra twenty words is ever a bad thing), you've practiced using your watch and self-pacing, and you've done a few full practice tests to build endurance. The focus of your test prep this week shouldn't be on studying for the test; it should be on preparing yourself mentally and physically so that you can wake up the morning of the test feeling your best. It doesn't matter how much studying you've done if you aren't in a condition to utilize that preparation during the test.

For mental preparation, stick to your daily meditations and "write it out" whenever you feel stressed. Channel your energy into reviewing a stack of previously completed practice tests. With the possible exception of Math or English/Writing sections, I would limit this review to official practice tests for consistency with the test you will see on Saturday. The beautiful thing about reviewing old practice tests is that there is zero pressure. You can either read through tests from beginning to end or you can focus specifically on the questions you answered incorrectly. Review any topics on which you lack clarity, note any careless mistakes that you don't want to make moving forward, and pat yourself on the back for all of the information you've learned since taking each practice test. Observe clues in the questions that point you to the right answer (ahem, these should be underlined, ahem, ahem). Take another stab at an impromptu essay.

Another aspect of your mental preparation has to do with familiarizing yourself with your commute to the test center. At some point during the week before the test, you should go to the center if you aren't familiar with its location. This will give you a sense of travel time and the confidence-boosting that you know how to get there. Also, take a look at your test prep playlist and spruce it up so you have some good tunes to listen to on the way to the test center.

Next, physical prep. In my opinion, physical prep is the single most important element to your routine the week before the test.

First and foremost, physical prep requires maintaining good sleeping habits the full week before the test. Each evening, give yourself the opportunity to unwind so that you can fall asleep with your body's natural rhythms. Your body sends you clues that it wants to fall asleep, but it is easy to ignore these impulses because that YouTube video is so funny or you want to make progress on your English paper. By looking at computer and television screens, you confuse your internal clock. Focus on completing your homework so that you can turn off electronics by 9 pm and be in bed by 10 pm. You don't need to stop working at 9, but try to be done with any homework that requires you to look at a computer screen. If you can't go to bed before 10:30, that's fine, but do your best.

My student Jack nodded at this advice and then proceeded to ignore it. Instead, he maintained his regular late-night routine early in the week and tried to compensate by going to bed extra early the night before the test. Guess what: it didn't work. Even though Jack went to bed, he couldn't sleep—not surprising since his body was accustomed to going to sleep later and he was experiencing pre-test jitters. Not to mention thinking that you can make up for, let's say, twenty hours of sleep deprivation (losing two hours of sleep a night for ten days) with an extra two hours of sleep in one night is unrealistic. You usually become sleep deprived over several days; similarly, you need several days to recover.

In addition to replenishing your sleep tank, try to maintain your regular exercise schedule and, if you don't already have a power breakfast that you love, experiment with different breakfasts, monitoring your energy levels throughout the morning.

If you are scheduling in your time the week before the test and are faced with the choice between running an extra practice drill and sleeping for an extra thirty minutes or going for a walk outside, choose the option that takes care of your physical well-being. Prioritizing how you feel physically will help you feel sharp and ready with your A-game on test day.

Why the Test Always Feels Harder on Test Day

A common concern when approaching an officially administered SAT or ACT is, "I've heard the official test is harder than the practice tests." This raises the question, why do students so often feel this way, and how do we mitigate the harder-on-test-day phenomenon?

First of all, let's consider the validity of the claim. Without discounting that the test seems harder or the effect that this perception can have on us, is it *true* that the test is harder on test day? As a coach, I've completed dozens of real SATs and ACTs, and I've yet to feel like one version of a test was significantly harder than the other versions. Maybe there are a few hard questions, but that's to be expected. So what is it that makes students perceive the test as harder? In a word: pressure.

Realistically, the test you will take on test day is about as difficult as any official test that you've practiced with. If you've followed the plan laid out in this book, before you arrive in the test room you will have already completed at least three official tests—one diagnostic and two or three practice tests. Any official test that you used to practice was once given to a room full of students like you, and these students probably thought that this version of the test was harder than any of the practice tests that they had previously seen. They made it through their test, and you'll make it through yours.

The good news is that the test is scored on a curve relative to the other test takers of that specific test. If this version of the test is objectively harder than the practice tests you took, the curve will reflect its difficulty. Furthermore, everyone is dealing with the "realness" of the test, and the curve reflects that, too. If anything, you have an advantage over most other test takers because you know (and hopefully practice) the centering techniques like meditation and stream-of-consciousness writing that I've taught you. These techniques will help you stay clear despite the pressure.

If the reason you perceive the test as harder on test day is because you feel more pressure on test day, you can reduce the harder-on-test-day phenomenon by changing how you relate to that pressure. Anytime the pressure starts to feel overwhelming, take a breath. If you are coming up against difficult questions, remember that you don't need to answer every question correctly to earn an excellent score, so it's okay if there are a few harder questions. Remember that if you've skillfully eliminated incorrect answers, there's a good chance that you will answer some of the harder questions correctly.

The best, most efficient test takers focus on solving problems, not creating them. The test is not a problem. It is what it is. Your only job is to answer as many questions correctly as possible. Stay focused on that, and you will be fine.

A Few Notes on Test-Day Nerves

Test takers often experience test-day nerves. It feels like a lot is on the line, and when the stakes are high, adrenaline surges. There's no single, definitive solution to nerves. Different mindsets and strategies will work for different people. Knowing that you have techniques that will help with nerves on the day of the test may help with nerves leading up to it. Here are a few to consider if you are dealing with nerves before the test begins.

Generalize the Experience

If you are someone who feels anxiety specifically around test taking, consider at least one other circumstance in which you feel nerves but don't let them get the best of you. This setting might be performing in a basketball game, a band concert, a dance recital, a debate, or a play performance, for example. You have the same quickening of your heart rate, the same thoughts of "I really want this to work out," the same keen awareness of your surroundings, the same uncertainty around what is about to transpire. Except in that other scenario, you don't judge the feeling as wrong. You allow the adrenaline to fuel your performance rather than hinder it.

You've experienced nerves before, but you didn't let them stop you. You can do the same thing in the test room.

This Is a Part of the Journey

You've been preparing for this. Remember what I said at the beginning? The test doesn't start on test day; it starts when you begin preparing for it. Likewise, this is probably not your last chance to take the SAT or ACT. Sure, it would be great if you knocked it out of the park and could cross college admissions tests off your to-do list, but if that's not the outcome of this test, it's okay. You will learn from your test-day experience, and you can apply those lessons moving forward.

Today's test is one step along your journey. It is not necessarily a determinant of how well you will ultimately do on the test or what college you will attend. Your score will simply reflect how you performed on today's test.

C'est la Vie

Confidence comes from knowing that you have prepared. Once you've given your best effort to the preparation process, you can walk into the test center and think, *"C'est la vie."* You've worked enough, thought enough, and done enough. Move forward with confidence. Let your worries go. Let your attachment to specific results go. Let it all go. Release all of the stored emotion, anticipation, and expectations so that you can be present while taking the test.

College admissions. Formulas. Pressure from parents. What your friends will think. Your future. *C'est la vie.*

Visualizations

Here are two useful visualizations for test day. Close your eyes, take a few breaths, then bring the visualization to mind.

If you feel stressed, imagine all of your anxiety as an iron weight that's pressing into your shoulders. Now, imagine it growing lighter and lighter until it floats away. All that's left is you and the test. Nothing else matters.

If you want to charge up, you can visualize the magical rain shower of SAT/ACT points that I introduced in "Meditation." Imagine that every point that falls on you further energizes you. This rain shower can also wash away any excess negativity.

Let Your Writing Be Your Guide

See if there are any wise words from that quiet, confident voice inside as you stream-of-consciousness write. Your inner guide speaks to you in a way that shines light on your fears, allowing you to address them and feel relief. As you write, open yourself to the possibility of finding the words that will comfort, motivate, or ground you. Write down the words that occur to you which corroborate this intention. Whatever support you need is there, if you listen for it.

Self-Talk

If anxiety comes up during the test, you can use one of the strategies that we discussed in "Self-Talk" (Chapter 1). In addition...

Leave Room for Miracles

We've all experienced the feeling that comes up when we read a problem and our mind draws a blank. A default response may be to tense up or to chastise yourself, but there's another option: leave room for miracles.

What if doing well on the test weren't all up to you? What if, as my college psychology professor half-jokingly suggested, there were angels sitting next to you as you took the test? Or what if the universe could "drop" an insight into your head on how to solve the problem?

If that were the case, I can almost guarantee you that the insights wouldn't come if you tensed up. Tension leaves no open space, and without open space, there's nowhere for the inspiration to enter. The easiest and most effective way to release tension: take a breath.

You can tweak these metaphors so that they fit into a framework that makes sense to you. Imagine your best friend or favorite teacher or dog sitting beside you. Choose an image that provides you with a greater sense of warmth, comfort, and ease.

Test-Day Eve

The night before the test, gather everything you will need for the test. Do not wait until the next morning. See the College Board and ACT websites for specifics regarding what is allowed in the test room. The list of things to bring includes, but is not limited to:

- Your admission ticket

- Photo ID

- Sharpened #2 pencils (mechanical pencils aren't permitted)

- Pencil sharpener

- Extra erasers (test them out in advance—some erasers leave streaks)

- Calculator with fresh batteries

- Snacks (I recommend nuts and an apple or a peanut butter and jelly/banana sandwich—think of a combination of carbs, fats, and protein)

- Floss (in case a bit of apple gets stuck in your teeth)

- Water

- Gum

- Tissues

- The clothes you will wear, plus an extra layer (you don't know what temperature the room will be)

- Car keys, metro card, sunglasses...whatever you need to physically travel to the test center

- Your test-friendly digital watch (come to think of it, put this on the night before)

Set your alarm. Heck, set two alarms. When you wake up, you should be able to function on autopilot because everything is organized and ready to go.

Program Your Day

Another activity that you can do the night before the test is what I call "programming your day." To program your day, take a notebook and write out how you want the next day to go. When you write, be specific. Don't write it like a grocery list—use adjectives and adverbs that create positive feelings. If you want to wake up energized, to have a smooth commute, and to move through the test with confidence, say so!

To give an example from my life, the night before the photo shoot for this book's cover, I wrote, "My alarm will go off and I will awaken well rested. I will joyfully meditate. I will have a delicious breakfast and green juice. I will have a smooth commute. I have a team of people supporting me. I move through life with great ease."

The next morning, I felt great. I knew exactly what I needed to do because I'd mentally rehearsed it the night before, and all of those adjectives and adverbs infused even the actions that are part of my standard morning routine with a little more fun and excitement. A few kind people even offered to carry my heavy suitcase (filled with everything I needed for the shoot) up the subway stairs, which certainly helped me to "move through life with great ease." Assert that you will feel exactly the way you want to feel every step of the way and see how it affects the flow of your morning.

Your Inner Four-Year-Old

Have you ever babysat a four-year-old? If you have, you know that even though they think they always know what's up...they don't. You have to take extra good care of four-year-olds to keep them happy, and that means planning ahead.

A four-year-old doesn't tell you to bring a sweatshirt on the chance that the air-conditioned room is set to 65 degrees—you bring it in case she feels cold.

A four-year-old doesn't tell you he will feel hungry in a few hours —you pack a snack, so that the minute he feels hungry, you have something to feed him.

A four-year-old doesn't tell you she has to go to the bathroom— you instruct her to go before she has to hold it.

On test day, take care of your inner four-year-old. Set everything up the night before. Bring a sweater and a snack. Go to the bathroom at every single opportunity (after you arrive at the test center and during the break), regardless of whether it feels like you have to—I cannot stress this last point enough; there are few distractions so maddening as a full bladder, and the last thing you want is to compromise your performance because of something so preventable. (I wouldn't emphasize this if I hadn't had students run into this exact problem during practice tests, even after we'd discussed it.)

And if your inner-four-year-old feels nervous? Reassure him or her that you are taking care of everything, and it will all be okay.

CHAPTER 11
TEST DAY AND AFTERMATH

This is the moment.

In this chapter, I will give you a strategy for test day. Then, I'll give you guidance on how to proceed once you've emerged from the test room. We'll talk about waiting for your scores, how to approach the sometimes sensitive issue of receiving your scores so that you feel grounded and secure, and how to decide whether to retake the test.

Test Day!

Congrats! You made it to test day! Go in and kick butt!

No matter what your usual patterns, eat a good breakfast. You have four hours of testing ahead of you, and you haven't eaten since dinner the night before. Food = body fuel = brain fuel. If you are accustomed to caffeine in the morning, have a small cup of coffee or tea—enough to boost your alertness, but not so much that your knee will be bouncing under your desk.

Plan to leave for the test center early. Ridiculously early. There might be traffic. You need to find a parking spot. The proctor will check IDs. You want time to stream-of-consciousness write. After all the effort you've invested into test preparation, you certainly don't want to feel stressed during your commute or risk being refused admission to take the test because you are running late.

Arriving early means that you will have at least fifteen minutes in the room before the test begins. At this point, you don't need to review formulas, because you've learned them. Sure, you could make nervous chitchat with the person sitting next to you, but is there anything that you can do that will help your performance?

Take the downtime you have before the test to focus and center yourself. Close your eyes or look down at a spot on your desk, and bring your attention to your breath.

Phew!

You made it through the official test. Yay, you!

The first thing you probably want to do is sleep. Or, if not sleep, maybe go to lunch with a friend or zone out in front of the television for a few hours. Whatever the next item on your to-do list, I highly recommend taking fifteen minutes to stream-of-consciousness write after the test, as you did beforehand.

Write down everything you remember from the test. How you felt, where you got stuck, where you were jamming, any questions or topics that left you with a sense of uncertainty. You don't need to do anything with your notes right away, but they might help you as you prepare for the next test or serve as a frame of reference when you receive your scores in a few weeks. It all feels fresh and unforgettable immediately after the test, but by the next day, your recollections won't be as sharp. Take time to reflect while the details are still clear.

The Deceptive Nature of Feelings

Don't take anyone's assessment of the test, including your own, as an objective truth. How many times have you taken a practice test and found that an educated guess turned out to be the correct answer? Probably many, whether you are aware of it or not—though I hope in your test prep you've been reviewing the educated-guess problems along with the problems you answered flat-out incorrectly. On the flip side, I'm sure there have been instances when you were shocked to discover you had answered a question incorrectly, and upon reviewing your work, realized that you had made a careless error.

After leaving the test room, some students want to debrief with their friends. There are certainly benefits to this: it's a good way to let off steam and compare impressions. That said, don't obsess. Recognize that after the test, all you or anyone is left with are feelings. Give yourself a little time to talk about it, and then move on.

You could feel awful about the test, but maybe it didn't turn out so badly. You could feel awesome about the test, but maybe you made careless mistakes. The same applies to your friends.

When you hear your friends say that they knocked it out of the park or that they couldn't have done any worse, smile and nod and tell them that it will be interesting to see what happens when the scores come out. When you hear chatter in your own head about the outcome of the test, tell yourself the same thing.

If you don't want to talk about the test with your friends, that's fine, too. If that's the case, I'd recommend communicating this to your friends prior to taking the test. When you establish your boundaries in advance, your friends won't be surprised when you hold to them—and your friends will also be less likely to bring up the test with you in the first place.

The Waiting Game

Okay, it's the next day. The hard part is over... Or is it?

After all, you have to wait for the scores.

Maybe you aren't thinking about your pending scores most of the time, but occasionally they cross your mind. You might experience a flutter of excitement-mixed-with-nerves, a wave of adrenaline, or nausea.

The best advice I have for you is the same advice I offer about taking the test itself: keep moving.

If you have the option of taking the test again, don't wait to find out your scores before resuming your test prep. You may not receive scores until a couple of weeks before the next test, after the registration deadline. If taking the test again is an option, plan to take it. Register for it. Prep for it. Prep in the same way you did for the previous one, except with greater insight, since you have clearer expectations about the experience for which you are preparing. You will feel better taking the test again if you haven't lost any time in preparing for your next official test.

The suggestion to keep moving holds even if you don't plan to take the test again. By continuing to take actions that serve your goals —such as performing well in school and activities and developing your college apps—you will feel better about your progress.

Of course, you may want to take a couple of days off from your test prep. That's fine. It's good to give yourself breathing room. If you do take time off, don't wait more than a week after the official test to resume your prep—schedule in your next session, and honor that commitment. You'd be surprised how quickly you fall out of practice. I've seen it happen, and I don't want you to lose the skills you've worked to acquire.

Another item for your after-the-test to-do list:

Both the SAT and ACT offer services through which, on certain test dates, you can order a copy of the test you took and a list of your answers. Take advantage of this offering when it is available! It allows you to observe where you need more work and where you are on the right track. For instructions on ordering your test booklet, visit the tests' respective websites.

Score Cancellation

If you didn't feel great about the official test, you may be considering canceling your scores.

Don't.

If this seems obvious, skip to the next section. If you need more convincing, read on.

You can only cancel your SAT and ACT scores before the scores have been released. Canceling your scores stops the scoring process. Beyond preventing schools from seeing your scores, a cancellation request stops you from receiving any results: no scores, no answer sheet, no test booklet.

So long as both the SAT and the ACT have the options of Score Choice and most colleges use Super Scoring, there is no benefit to canceling test scores. If you obliterate record of the test, you lose any insights from that test day. By seeing your scores, you can compare the outcome to your impressions.

As we previously discussed, feelings can be misleading. They don't always reflect the truth of a situation. You may not have performed as badly as you imagine you did—and that would be good to find out. If the score does align with your impression, you will take a breath and move on. You will continue your prep work. You will continue to do your best. You will dedicate yourself to this process in the service of your dreams and ambitions. You aren't a failure—you have some scores that you will never show anyone. So what?

If you receive your scores, you are a person who didn't run away. You viewed your scores and said, "Okay, good to know. Let's keep moving." Nothing fazed you. Or, you let yourself feel it for a bit, and then reached a point mentally and emotionally when you were ready to move on, sooner rather than later. This is what the leaders of the world do—whether creative, entrepreneurial, athletic, philanthropic, inventive, or some combination thereof. Leaders see things as they are and keep working to transform them into how they could be. This is an opportunity for you to do just that.

MYOS (Mind Your Own Scores)

If you feel anxious about receiving your scores, one of the reasons may be that you are worried about what others will think when they hear your results. If that's the case, this advice may help to alleviate your discomfort.

Don't discuss your scores with your classmates. Here's the thing: your scores are nobody else's business. By the same token, other people's scores are none of your business. Your scores won't make your classmates' scores any higher or lower nor will they affect where your friends get into college. They are *your* results and they were determined by *your* performance on the test. Let others deal with their scores and you deal with yours.

One of my high school friends didn't discuss her scores. She was smart, and I'm sure she did well. But even more impressive than knowing her specific scores was the quiet confidence with which she declined to comment on them. By gracefully setting clear boundaries, she acted out of self-respect, which was met by respect from her peers. She had nothing to prove.

If you choose not to discuss your results, in advance of receiving your scores you can let your friends know that you have no intention of discussing the results. Once the scores are issued, if a classmate happens to ask how you did, you can simply say, "I'm not discussing my scores."

If you set these boundaries, you need to follow through. If you find out that you scored well, don't brag about it to everyone who will listen—and you will definitely find a captive audience among your classmates. Similarly, if you didn't score as well as you wanted, don't go crying or complaining about it publicly. Finally, don't ask classmates about their scores, if you have decided not to discuss your own.

Maybe you will choose to share your scores with a few confidantes (including your parents and your tutor, if you have one), but choose these people wisely. Be particularly careful about confiding in someone from your high school—including your best friend—because everyone with whom you share your scores has the power to tell them to someone else. If word does spread, either directly or indirectly from you, you will have less credibility with others the next time you take the test and scores are released. Integrity is the result of your actions and words matching up. If you say you want one thing and then act in a way that's inconsistent with your assertion, it will confuse the people around you. They won't know how to treat you.

Above all, remember, your worth is not dependent on how you score, much less on other people's perceptions of your score.

Discussing Scores with Your Parents

While you may not want to share your scores with your peers, you should feel free to discuss your scores with your parents. No matter what the results are, let your parents support you and share in your journey.

If you are feeling anxious about sharing the results, you can feel more in control of conversations regarding the test by talking with your parents a few days before the scores are released. In this case, you can say something like, "The ACT/SAT scores are coming out in a few days. I have every intention of sharing them with you, but I want to do so on my terms. Please give me the time and space I need. I will come to you when I am ready to discuss them."

Of course, you may tell your parents your results within five minutes of learning your scores. You may want your parents next to you when you check your results online. But by talking to your parents ahead of time, you set the expectation that the process of checking and communicating your scores will go however you want it to go on the day the scores are released.

Interpreting Interquartile Ranges

All right, it's time. Let's talk about your scores and what they mean in the context of college admissions.

Every college admissions office releases the interquartile range (IQR) of the standardized test scores of their incoming freshman class. The IQR defines the 25th to the 75th percentile of accepted students' scores. This means that 25 percent of accepted students performed better than the higher number in the range and 25 percent performed worse than the lower number in the range. Colleges don't set official minimum scores that a student must earn to be considered for admission, but the IQR is a great way to gauge how your scores compare to those of other applicants.

No score on the SAT or ACT will guarantee you a spot at a given college. Schools like Harvard reject students with perfect scores. This is a reality of the admissions process. Your goal shouldn't be to score highly enough to earn admission to a particular school; your goal should be to earn a score that doesn't detract from your application. The latter objective generally means scoring above the 50th percentile for a given school. But remember that, by definition, 50 percent of an incoming class scored below that.

The raw score that translates to a specific scaled score will vary slightly among test dates because of the curve. However, when using official material, you easily see how your score compares using their conversion charts. You can also use one of these charts to get a sense of how many questions you would need to answer correctly on future tests to earn your target score.

Standardized test scores are a piece of the admissions puzzle, just like your GPA, essays, interviews, extracurriculars, internships, and awards and honors are pieces of the puzzle. While your admissions test scores may not reach all-star levels, you can still come across as an all-star because of other aspects of your application.

Should You Retake the Test?

There's no magic number for how many times you should take the SAT or ACT. Many students benefit from taking the test three times. That allows a student one test run and two full runs. The more times you take the test, the more experience you have. Regardless, at some point you will either have to decide to stop, or you will reach the final test date for which scores will be considered by college admissions officers (in which case, your decision to stop becomes super easy!).

Previously, we established that one of the goals of preparing for the test is to reach the point where you can confidently say, *"C'est la vie"* to yourself before the test. That's also your goal with your scores.

Your confidence has reached the level at which you decide that if a college rejects you because of your scores, then it wasn't the right college for you. You'll never know exactly why a school didn't offer you a place in its freshman class. Maybe it had nothing to do with your scores. It's the nature of college admissions: if not everyone can be accepted into a freshman class, many well-deserving students will be denied admission. But if you've reached the point with your scores at which you can say, "This is me. These are my scores. Take it or leave it," then you've won.

CHAPTER 12

CLOSING THOUGHTS

You've made it this far in the book, which means that you are ready to rock the remainder of your test prep. You've positioned yourself well for success on the tests and beyond.

But before I send you on your way, I have some parting thoughts...

It All Works Out

Chances are that when you brainstormed goals at the beginning of the book, those goals included admission to a college you want to attend. Maybe you had one specific college in mind, or maybe you simply had a general sense of how it would feel to be somewhere great.

When I applied to colleges, Princeton was my dream school. My father had attended Princeton, and it was one of the only colleges I had ever visited. Memories of reunion weekend mixed with high rankings in *U.S. News & World Report* and the promise of talented peers and accomplished professors to create an image of an idyllic college haven. Princeton epitomized everything I wanted my undergraduate experience to be. It held the keys to my castle.

Since you've read about my college experience in Chapter 1, you know that I graduated from Georgetown. Not Princeton.

While the seventeen-year-old inside me would love to tell you that I was accepted to Princeton and, upon visiting the different schools, decided that Georgetown was the better fit, that is not the case. The reality is that I was wait-listed, and, ultimately, never offered a spot at Princeton. But I was accepted to Georgetown and several other top universities.

During my freshman year at Georgetown, when things weren't going perfectly, I returned to my fantasy of how great things would have been at Princeton. I considered applying elsewhere as a transfer student, but always opted against it, wanting to make Georgetown work, tending my own garden instead of admiring how green the grass was on the other side of the fence.

By the time I was a senior at Georgetown, my brother was beginning his freshman year of college…at Princeton. As I spoke with him and heard about his college experience and compared it to my own, I realized that Georgetown was, in fact, the better fit for me. This is nothing against Princeton, but my brother's college experience was the right one for him, and mine was the right one for me.

Georgetown's unique sensibility and approach to learning worked well for me. It turns out that being rejected by Princeton University was for the best. Sometimes I like to imagine that the Princeton admissions officer evaluating my application hadn't eaten in a few hours and was feeling cranky and a little light-headed. It wasn't that my application didn't warrant an acceptance letter; it was merely that the admissions officer's hunger clouded his or her good judgment. How lucky for me that this was the case, because had I received an acceptance letter from Princeton, there's no way I would have attended Georgetown in light of the fantasy I had created about life at Princeton.

Furthermore, given my success at Georgetown, you'd be hard-pressed to convince me that I would have done any less than stellar at Princeton or many other undergraduate programs in the U.S. Remember that one school's opinion of the two-dimensional paper version of you is not a definitive judgment of you or of your potential. In fact, no one's opinion has that kind of power.

Trust that no matter what you think your top choice is as you submit your applications, the right school for you will offer you admission, and it may or may not be the one that you had dreamed of attending. The best result that you can hope for is that the admissions officer at your *real* dream school will be well fed, well rested, and ready to be dazzled as he or she picks up your application.

And, should you end up generally unhappy with your college choice, for whatever reason, you can always transfer.

Take Your Happy Ending for Granted

Once, when I was at a major decision point during a not-so-fun period of my early twenties (they happen), my brother gave me a magical piece of advice. He said, "What if you could take for granted that it all works out? However you would want to proceed, do that."

Imagine if every step you took were a step in a positive direction. It wouldn't merely all work out someday, but rather it's all working out right now, already.

Imagine if you could take your happy ending for granted.

Of course, you would try your best, because that's what people do when they are working toward a goal. But whatever the outcome of your efforts, you'd know that you are moving in a positive direction.

You Get Out What You Put In

Wherever you end up for college, it is important to remember that what you get out of an experience is proportional to what you put into it.

No matter where you attend college, there will be opportunities to engage. Engage with classes, activities, causes, ideas, and interests. Be curious, think harder, imagine bigger, discover more.

No matter where you attend college, there will be great professors. Find them. Be willing to wake up a little earlier if it means taking a great professor's class. Visit them during office hours. Ask questions. Listen to the answers.

No matter where you attend college, there will be the possibility of friendships. Get out there. Meet people. Participate in activities that are meaningful to you. Take classes that excite you. Through pursuing your interests and engaging your passions, you will meet like-minded people.

No matter where you attend college, there will be people you don't jam with. That's fine. Let them be friends with someone else. Continue seeking out the people who are more on your wavelength. They are there.

No matter where you attend college, there will be food and there will be roads. Eat the food. Run the roads, or engage in some other physical activity. Exercise will keep you sane…and compensate for hitting the cafeteria buffet a little too hard at brunch. The student-run coffee house will probably sell bagels and mint mochas. I recommend choosing to indulge in them one at a time. If you eat both, you will be hungry again in an hour.

No matter where you attend college, there will be ups and downs. The downs will make you stronger. The ups will be your reward for persevering through the downs.

No matter where you attend college, your journey is with yourself. The college and the people there will help shape your experience, but in the end it is about you. Take initiative. Follow your heart. Do what feels right, and let the rest go.

Applying What You've Learned to the Rest of Your Life

Getting out of an experience what you put into it isn't the only lesson that carries over from test prep to the rest of your life. Over the course of your test prep, what have you discovered about yourself? The way you learn? The way you manage time? The way you deal with pressure or resistance? How you define your self-worth? How you find peace amidst the chaos?

There is a saying, "What is in the one is in the whole." How you negotiate any challenge will both inform and mirror how you relate to other aspects of your life. By opening yourself to seeing these connections, you will find lessons that will serve you beyond the moment you receive your score report.

One of My Favorite Paradoxes

A paradox is a statement that seems contradictory but is nonetheless true. For example, that which seems big is really small, and that which seems small is really big.

Chances are, your college admissions test feels really big to you right now. And, in some ways, maybe it is. But in a lot of ways, it's actually quite small. Ten years from now, you'll remember little of your testing experience. You'll remember studying (or, more specifically, you'll remember that you studied). You'll vaguely remember sitting in a room with other test takers. You'll remember the general shape of the test books, but you won't remember the questions written in them. You may or may not remember your scores. You'll definitely remember if the drum line was rehearsing outside the test center as you took the test. You'll know where you went to college. You'll remember your college experience. But the standardized test part of the admissions process? Foggy, if not forgotten.

You're more likely to remember your favorite concert. The teacher who changed the way you think about life and learning. Your pet greeting you when you walked in the door, and sitting with you when you were home on a Friday night. The person who was kind even though you barely knew him or her. Someone who smiled or supported you on a bad day. The time you helped a struggling classmate. Achieving a goal that you had hoped for but didn't expect to realize. Not achieving a goal that you'd worked hard for, but also not letting the disappointment stop you, continuing to work, and achieving bigger things down the line.

These are the moments that we remember in life.

That which seems big is really small; that which seems small is really big.

ACKNOWLEDGMENTS

There may be only one name on the cover of this book, but it truly takes a village, and I wouldn't have it any other way.

Thanks to Madison Jones and Joshua Oppenheimer for reading drafts, providing insights, and encouraging me to keep going when I was facing my own internal resistance. Josh, your wisdom, humor, and compassion enrich my life. Madison, you are savvy, witty, generous, and a 99th percentile friend.

Thanks to Steven Sabat, Daniel Porterfield, Anthony Arend, Mary Halseth, Wayne Knoll, William Esper, and many other amazing teachers for opening my mind and broadening my perspective. Special thanks to Thomas Lubeck for not only challenging and impacting me as a teacher, but also for reading and providing feedback on an early draft of this book.

Thanks to Lauren Toub for her rockstar-worthy photography (and friendship), Krishna Fitzpatrick for turning my doodles into design, and Amy Scott for her thoughtful edits.

Jennifer Gleason-Wilson, you have been a mentor and a major source of support to me. Thank you.

ACKNOWLEDGMENTS

Thank you to Rich Rowe, Kayla Hines, Traci Hines, Hilary Pearlson, Barb Schmidt, Michele Kambolis, and Daisy Barth for the support, kindness, and generosity you offered me during the book creation process. I appreciate you so much.

Jackie Sokol, you are a beautiful presence in my life and I'm so grateful for our friendship.

I am ever grateful to Emily Nakkawita for the kindness, clarity, and warmth she brings to every conversation. Emily was my freshman-year roommate at Georgetown. We didn't make the best roommates at eighteen, but she continues to be one of my dearest friends ten years later. Remember this if you hit a speed bump in your relationship with your roommate: there's still hope!

I hit the yoga mat at Katonah Yoga almost every day during the time I spent working on this book. Thank you to Melissa French, Abbie Galvin, Nevine Michaan, Charlotte Price, Jenna Sisson, and the rest of the community for your friendship and guidance.

In the book, I reference my Vedic meditation practice. I was first taught this form of meditation by Thom Knoles and receive ongoing guidance from Emily Fletcher and other Vedic meditation teachers. Their teachings on meditation and life are exciting, resonant, and transformative.

Thanks to my students. Your vulnerability, willingness, and determination are incredibly inspiring and it is my absolute pleasure to work with you. You've each left an imprint on my heart.

Special thanks to my parents, Mark and Matilda Oppenheimer. You have supported me every step of the way, and I'm filled with gratitude for and admiration of each of you.

LET'S CONNECT

If you want to receive more tips from me about the test prep process, you can sign up for email updates on my website, **www.erikaoppenheimer.com**. I'll email you every time I post something new on my blog, where I expand on the topics covered in this book. I also share free bonuses with subscribers, such as my three-part *Organize Your Test Prep* email and PDF series.

Find my Facebook page at **www.fb.erikaoppenheimer.com** and connect with me on Twitter at **@erika_opp**. When you do something that makes you feel a sense of achievement, tag me and use the hashtag **#AcingIt**. That way I can celebrate with you!

Feel free to email me at **erika@erikaoppenheimer.com**. Students like you are why I do this. I would love to hear your response to the book. You may also email me if you are interested in individual or group coaching.

Keep up the good work!

Erika

Made in the USA
Middletown, DE
24 October 2015